Integrating Instruction

in

Language Arts

Strategies, Activities, Projects, Tools, and Techniques

by Imogene Forte and Sandra Schurr

Incentive Publications, Inc.
Nashville, Tennessee

Illustrated by Marta Drayton
Cover by Geoffrey Brittingham
Edited by Jan Keeling

ISBN 0-86530-323-1

PRINTED IN THE UNITED STATES OF AMERICA

TABLE OF CONTENTS

PREFACE 7–8

Using Integrated Instructional Strategies to Accommodate Differing Learning Styles, Abilities, and Interests

Using Multiple Intelligences as an Instructional Tool

OVERVIEW

Multiple Intelligences: Overview 10–11

ACTIVITY PAGES

Book Reports   Be a Book Reporter 12

Grammar   Parts of Speech 13

Poetic Terms   Poetry 14

Punctuation   Punctuation Rules 15

Public Speaking   Join the Speaker's Bureau 16

Plural Nouns   Forming Plurals for Practice 17

Reference Materials   Using Multiple Resources to Find Answers 18–19

Writing/Technology   Word Processor Wisdom 20

Proverbs   Proverbs Are Wise Sayings 21

Creative Communications   Creative Writing, Thinking, and Speaking 22

Listening Skills   The Payoffs of Active Listening 23

Using Learning Stations as an Instructional Tool

OVERVIEW

Learning Stations: Overview 24–28

Using Integrated Instructional Strategies to Develop Problem-solving and Higher-order Thinking Skills

Using Bloom's Taxonomy as an Instructional Tool

Bloom's Taxonomy: Overview 30–31

ACTIVITY PAGES

Parts of Speech	Verb Review	32
Poetry	Poetry Pickup	33
Journalism	News and Views	34
Test Taking	A Takeoff on Tests	35
Storytelling	Storytelling	36
Editing Process	Editor's Guidelines	37
Biography/Autobiography	A View of You	38–40
Literature	For Fiction's Sake	41

Using Williams' Taxonomy as an Instructional Tool

Williams' Taxonomy: Overview 42–43

ACTIVITY PAGES

Language Arts	Pasta Perfect	44–45
Listening Skills	Listening In	46–47
Reference Materials	Reference Referral	48–49

Using Investigation Cards as an Instructional Tool

Investigation Cards: Overview 50

INVESTIGATION CARDS

Word Usage	Investigate the Magic of Language	51–54
Alphabets/Codes	Investigate the Alphabet	55–58
Literature	Investigate a Book of Fiction	59–62
Reference Materials	Investigate a Dictionary	63–66

Using Calendars as an Instructional Tool

Using Calendars: Overview 67–68

CALENDARS

Word Usage	Word Power	69
Public Speaking	Speak Up	70
Creativity	Use Your Imagination . . .	71
Publishing	Personal Publishing Project	72

Using Integrated Instructional Strategies to Promote Cooperative Learning and Group Interaction

OVERVIEW

Using Cooperative Learning as an Instructional Tool 74–79

COOPERATIVE LEARNING ACTIVITIES

Think/Pair/Share   Language Arts Activities 80–85

Three-step Interview   Folklore 86–90

Circle of Knowledge   Language Arts Activities 91–96

Team Learning   Fun with Words 97–101

Co-op Co-op   Gods and Goddesses of Mount Olympus 102–103

Numbered Heads   Paragraph Power 104–105

Round Table   Literary Analysis 106–115

Jigsaw Activity   Poetry Portraits 116–118

Using Integrated Instructional Strategies to Facilitate Authentic Assessment

OVERVIEW

Authentic Assessment: Overview 120–121

JOURNAL WRITING

Journal Writing Guidelines 122–123

Springboards for Journal Writing 124–126

OTHER SPRINGBOARDS

Springboards for Student Products 127–128

Springboards for Student Performances 129–130

SAMPLE PORTFOLIO

Interdisciplinary Unit in Language Arts 131–140

A Very Practical Appendix

INTERDISCIPLINARY INSTRUCTION

Integrating Instruction through Planning and Carrying
out a Language Arts Festival 142–143

Ten High-interest Strategies/Activities to Integrate
Social Studies into Language Arts 144–145

Ten High-interest Strategies/Activities to
Integrate Science into Language Arts 146–147

Ten High-interest Strategies/Activities to
Integrate Math into Language Arts 148–149

PLANNING OUTLINES

Editor's Guide 150

Outline for Interdisciplinary Unit in Language Arts .. 151

Integrating Language Arts to Accommodate
Multiple Intelligences 152

Integrating Language Arts to Accommodate
Williams' Taxonomy 153

Book Report Ladder 154

Book Report Outline for Use with Any Topic 155

BIBLIOGRAPHY

Annotated Bibliography 156–157

INDEX 158–159

Preface

Middle grades educators are meeting the challenges of student-centered education with new teaching methods to create a positive learning climate for students in early adolescence. Middle grades language arts educators want to know how to use these new instructional strategies and organizational procedures in ways that are specifically designed for their classes.

Integrating Instruction in Language Arts was created especially for language arts educators at the middle grade level. The high-interest activities cover topics in important areas in language arts, including:

- Creative writing
- Editing
- Fiction
- Folklore and myth
- Grammar and punctuation
- Journal writing
- Language and word usage
- Literary criticism

- Nonfiction
- Parts of speech
- Poetry
- Reference materials
- Speaking and listening
- Storytelling
- Taking tests
- Vocabulary

In each of five major sections is a comprehensive overview of a particular instructional focus accompanied by stimulating activities that are meant to be used as well as to serve as examples.

USING INTEGRATED INSTRUCTIONAL STRATEGIES TO ACCOMMODATE DIFFERING LEARNING STYLES, ABILITIES, AND INTERESTS features guidelines for incorporating the Multiple Intelligences and learning stations into the preparation of high-quality lesson plans and student assignments.

USING INTEGRATED INSTRUCTIONAL STRATEGIES TO DEVELOP PROBLEM-SOLVING AND HIGHER-ORDER THINKING SKILLS offers guidelines for infusing higher-order thinking skills into the educational process through the use of cognitive taxonomies, self-directed investigation cards, and calendars. The cognitive taxonomies offer useful foundations for the design of interdisciplinary units, student worksheets, learning stations, and group projects.

USING INSTRUCTIONAL STRATEGIES TO PROMOTE COOPERATIVE LEARNING AND GROUP INTERACTION presents valuable collaborative processes such as Think/Pair/Share, Three-step Interview, Circle of Knowledge, Team Learning, Co-op Co-op, Numbered Heads Together, Round Table, and Jigsaw.

USING INTEGRATED INSTRUCTIONAL STRATEGIES TO FACILITATE AUTHENTIC ASSESSMENT shows how to effectively implement product, performance, and portfolio assessment practices. Included is a complete sample portfolio based on an interdisciplinary unit in language arts.

Finally, **A VERY PRACTICAL APPENDIX** provides high-interest strategies and activities to integrate social studies, science, and math into the language arts curriculum; topics for student reports and journal writing; blank planning outlines to help in the creation of original lesson plans; and an annotated bibliography. A comprehensive index will make it easy to keep track of this wealth of information.

In short, this book is a must for all language arts educators, for those on interdisciplinary teams as well as those in self-contained classrooms. It offers a collection of instructional strategies that were designed for heterogeneous groups of students in an educational setting that will allow every student to be successful. It clarifies theoretical principles and offers activities that cover a wide range of important topics in language arts. Best of all, its content is fresh, original, and of interest to contemporary middle grades students.

Using Integrated Instructional Strategies to Accommodate Differing Learning Styles, Abilities, and Interests

USING MULTIPLE INTELLIGENCES
AS AN INSTRUCTIONAL TOOL
Overview 10
Be a Book Reporter 12
Parts of Speech 13
Poetry 14
Punctuation Rules 15
Join the Speaker's Bureau 16
Forming Plurals for Practice 17
Using Multiple Resources to Find Answers 18
Word Processor Wisdom 20
Proverbs Are Wise Sayings 21
Creative Writing, Thinking, and Speaking 22
The Payoffs of Active Listening 23
USING LEARNING STATIONS
AS AN INSTRUCTIONAL TOOL
Overview 24

Using Multiple Intelligences as an Instructional Tool

Howard Gardner's Theory of the Multiple Intelligences provides teachers with an excellent model for the design of interdisciplinary units, student worksheets, learning stations, and group projects. Gardner is quick to point out that (1) every student has at least one dominant intelligence (although he or she may have more than one); (2) these intelligences can all be nurtured, strengthened, and taught over time; (3) the intelligences do not exist in isolation but interface and interact with one another when a student is completing a task; and (4) the intelligences provide teachers with seven different ways to approach the curriculum. Gardner has identified and described seven major intelligences:

VERBAL/LINGUISTIC DOMINANCE
Students strong in this type of intelligence have highly developed verbal skills, and often think in words. They do well on written assignments, enjoy reading, and are good at communicating and expressing themselves.

LOGICAL/MATHEMATICAL DOMINANCE
Students strong in this intelligence think in abstractions and handle complex concepts, and they readily see patterns or relationships in ideas. They like to work with numbers and perform mathematical operations, and approach problem-solving exercises with logic and rational thought.

VISUAL/SPATIAL DOMINANCE
Students with visual/spatial strength think in images, symbols, colors, pictures, patterns, and shapes. They like to perform tasks that require "seeing with the mind's eye"—tasks that require them to visualize, imagine, pretend, or form images.

BODY/KINESTHETIC DOMINANCE
Students dominant in this intelligence have a strong body awareness and a sharp sense of physical movement. They communicate best through body language, physical gestures, hands-on activities, active demonstrations, and performance tasks.

MUSICAL/RHYTHMIC DOMINANCE
Students with this dominant intelligence enjoy music, rhythmic patterns, variations in tones or rhythms, and sounds. They enjoy listening to music, composing music, interpreting music, performing to music, and learning with music playing in the background.

INTERPERSONAL DOMINANCE

Students with this dominant intelligence thrive on person-to-person interactions and team activities. They are sensitive to the feelings and needs of others and are skilled team members, discussion leaders, and peer mediators.

INTRAPERSONAL DOMINANCE

Students with this dominant intelligence prefer to work alone because they are self-reflective, self-motivated, and in tune with their own feelings, beliefs, strengths, and thought processes. They respond to intrinsic rather than extrinsic rewards and may demonstrate great wisdom and insight when presented with personal challenges and independent study opportunities.

The Theory of Multiple Intelligences can be used as a guide for the teacher who is interested in creating lesson plans that address one or more of the intelligences on a daily basis. Teachers should ask themselves the following questions when attempting to develop or evaluate classroom activities using seven intelligences:

(1) What tasks require students to write, speak, or read?

(2) What tasks require students to engage in problem solving, logical thought, or calculations?

(3) What tasks require students to create images or visual aids and to analyze colors, textures, forms, or shapes?

(4) What tasks require students to employ body motions, manipulations, or hands-on approaches to learning?

(5) What tasks require students to incorporate music, rhythm, pitch, tones, or environmental sounds in their work?

(6) What tasks require students to work in groups and to interact with others?

(7) What tasks require students to express personal feelings, insights, beliefs, and self-disclosing ideas?

The following pages provide the teacher with several examples of how the Multiple Intelligences have been used as an organizing structure when designing classroom materials and assignments.

Using the Multiple Intelligences to

Be a Book Reporter

Complete the following set of activities in order to prepare a book report.

VERBAL/LINGUISTIC

In approximately 150 words or less, retell the important events or actions of the story. Write your summary or synopsis as it might appear on a book jacket.

LOGICAL/MATHEMATICAL

List five major events of the story and tell what caused each to happen. Present your work in two columns, one labeled EVENT, the other labeled WHAT CAUSED THE EVENT TO HAPPEN.

VISUAL/SPATIAL

Create a map, drawing, or diagram to show the main setting of the story. Be sure to include all of the special places where the action occurs. Label each important spot with a symbol and create a key or legend for your work.

BODY/KINESTHETIC

Create a postcard that could be sent by the main character of the story to the author of the book. Draw an interesting scene from the story on one side of the postcard; on the other side of the postcard, write a message that tells how the main character feels about the plot that the author created for him or her.

MUSICAL/RHYTHMIC

Pretend a famous television or movie producer wants to turn your book into a musical. List the major characters from the story. Decide which famous movie actor or actress you want for each part; tell why.

INTERPERSONAL

Prepare a two-minute speech about your book. Give the speech to a small group of peers. Ask each peer to rate your speech on a scale of 1 to 3 using the following criteria: a. delivery; b. information presented; c. organization of ideas; and d. interest generated in the story.

1 = Could be better   2 = Good   3 = Excellent

INTRAPERSONAL

Think about the values and ideas that are demonstrated by the main characters of the story. Write a paragraph summarizing these values. Tell if and how they relate to your own life and beliefs.

Grammar

Parts of Speech

VERBAL/LINGUISTIC
List the eight parts of speech and write a definition of each. Choose an interesting science or social studies topic (such as **weather** or **elections**) and write a comprehensive sentence on that topic that contains an example of each part of speech.

LOGICAL/MATHEMATICAL
Choose an interesting science or social studies topic (such as **plants** or **pioneers**). Write a paragraph containing examples of all the parts of speech on your selected topic. Underline and label each part of speech.

VISUAL/SPATIAL
Choose a science or social studies topic of interest to you (such as **magnetism** or **explorers**). Think of a key phrase or sentence that is related to that topic and that contains each part of speech. Draw a diagram of your phrase or sentence and label each part of speech.

BODY/KINESTHETIC
Look through the newspaper and find an article related to a science or social studies theme that is of special interest to you. Cut out the article and find in it examples of each part of speech. Paste the article on a sheet of paper and underline or label examples of nouns, pronouns, verbs, adjectives, adverbs, conjunctions, prepositions, and interjections.

MUSICAL/RHYTHMIC
Find lyrics to a song popular during an interesting historical period (examples: a **spiritual**, a **patriotic ballad**). Make eight columns, one for each part of speech. Place each word of the song in the correct column.

INTERPERSONAL
Select an interesting topic in science or social studies (such as **planets** or **Revolutionary War battles**). Locate the chapter in your textbook which relates to that topic and copy 25 to 50 sentences, underlining major parts of speech in each. Stage a "part of speech bee" (like a spelling bee), challenging a small group of peers to identify the part of speech of one or more of the underlined words in each sentence.

INTRAPERSONAL
Choose an interesting topic in science or social studies (such as **insects** or **government**). For each part of speech, think of a word related to your selected topic that has special meaning or significance to you.

Poetic Terms/Categories

Poetry

VERBAL/LINGUISTIC

Select a poem that you like that fits each of the following categories. Practice reading the poems aloud into a tape recorder, in front of a camcorder, or for a small group of peers:

1. Limerick
2. Ballad
3. Free Verse
4. Humorous or Nonsense Poem
5. Serious Poem
6. Sonnet

LOGICAL/MATHEMATICAL

Locate an example of each of the following types of figurative language in poems of your own choosing: **metaphor, simile, personification, alliteration, imagery, hyperbole,** and **onomatopoeia.** Set up four columns to record the information for each example.

Col. 1: Title of poem   Col. 3: Type of figurative language
Col. 2: Author of poem   Col. 4: Example of figurative language

VISUAL/SPATIAL

Locate a poem for each of the categories listed in the Logical/Mathematical activity. Copy these poems, illustrate them, and use them to make a poetry booklet. Include a cover, title page, and bibliography.

BODY/KINESTHETIC

Select a poem and choreograph a dance of movements to the poem. Have someone read the poem aloud while you perform the dance.

MUSICAL/RHYTHMIC

Meter refers to regular patterns of heavily and lightly stressed syllables. An accented syllable is a heavily stressed syllable in a poem. An unaccented syllable is a lightly stressed syllable in the metered poem. Select a poem for each of the categories listed in the Logical/Mathematical activity. Clap out the rhythm pattern for a stanza from each poem.

INTERPERSONAL

Work with a small group of peers to plan a "poetry reading" party for the class. Think of a special poetry theme for the party and create appropriate invitations, decorations, menu, and poetry reading/sharing activities.

INTRAPERSONAL

Create a **simile, metaphor, alliterative** statement, **hyperbole** statement, and an **imagery** statement—each one about yourself.

Punctuation

Punctuation Rules

VERBAL/LINGUISTIC
Write a set of punctuation rules for use of the **comma**, the **colon**, the **semicolon**, the **hyphen**, the **apostrophe**, and **quotation marks**.

LOGICAL/MATHEMATICAL
Compare and contrast the writing of two very different authors according to the types of sentence structure, dialogue, and types of punctuation they use. Write your conclusions in a paragraph, giving specific examples to support your ideas.

VISUAL/SPATIAL
Pick a short newspaper or magazine article to read. Use varied highlighter markers to "colorize" the different types of punctuation found in the selection.

BODY/KINESTHETIC
Practice reading and acting out a novel or textbook selection. Use body movements and physical gestures to depict the various types of punctuation in the selection.

MUSICAL/RHYTHMIC
Accompany a reading selection with appropriate sounds to depict various types of punctuation.

INTERPERSONAL
Design a punctuation drill exercise and perform it with a partner.

INTRAPERSONAL
Determine whether you are more like a comma, colon, semicolon, apostrophe, hyphen, or a pair of quotation marks. Give reasons for your choice.

Public Speaking

Join the Speaker's Bureau

VERBAL/LINGUISTIC

For each of the following types of speeches, prepare a list of topics that could be used by the speaker:

1. **Impromptu Speech**
2. **How-to or Demonstration Speech**
3. **Speech To Persuade**
4. **Speech To Inform**
5. **Speech To Entertain**
6. **Monologue**

LOGICAL/MATHEMATICAL

Prepare an outline that shows the points that should be covered in the introduction, body, and conclusion of a typical speech.

VISUAL/SPATIAL

Prepare a list of visual props or aids that one could use to make a speech more interesting and informative.

BODY/KINESTHETIC

Prepare a checklist that indicates how a speaker might use body language and a positive physical image to improve the delivery of his or her speech.

MUSICAL/RHYTHMIC

Make a list of ways a speaker could use music to enhance his or her speech performance, and a list of musical selections that could be used for this purpose.

INTERPERSONAL

Work with a partner to develop a set of assessment rubrics for each of the different types of speeches listed in the Verbal/Linguistic activity.

INTRAPERSONAL

Select one of the different types of speeches listed in the Verbal/Linguistic activity and prepare and deliver this type of speech about yourself or about a topic that has special meaning to you.

Plural Nouns

Forming Plurals for Practice

VERBAL/LINGUISTIC

Explain how to form plurals of the following:

a. most singular nouns

b. most nouns ending in **ch**, **s**, **sh**, **x**, or **z**

c. a noun ending in **y** preceded by a vowel

d. a noun ending in **y** preceded by a consonant

e. a noun ending in **f** preceded by a vowel

f. a noun ending in **o** preceded by a vowel

g. a noun ending in **o** preceded by a consonant

h. nouns ending in **o** preceded by a consonant that are exceptions to the rule above

i. nouns whose plurals are the same as the singular forms

j. noun plurals that are irregular and must be memorized

LOGICAL/MATHEMATICAL

Devise a survey, quiz, or questionnaire for class members to identify those rules for forming plurals of nouns that are most difficult to apply. Show your results in chart or graph form.

VISUAL/SPATIAL

Design an attractive, colorful, and informative "cheat sheet" that shows students the rules for forming plurals of nouns. Encourage them to keep this learning aid in their writing notebooks and to use it regularly.

BODY/KINESTHETIC

Create and act out a story or play in which the characters are plurals of nouns that have been formed in a variety of ways according to a number of rules, some of which are in conflict with one another.

MUSICAL/RHYTHMIC

Invent various humming patterns to accompany the rules for forming plurals of nouns.

INTERPERSONAL

Design a lesson plan that could be used to teach others about forming plurals of nouns according to an "each one teach one" plan.

INTRAPERSONAL

Determine how learning to form plurals of nouns correctly can improve your writing.

Reference Materials

Using Multiple Resources to Find Answers

Page 1

VERBAL/LINGUISTIC

Write a short position paper explaining how one could conduct research and locate information for a project using each of the following types of resources:

1. Visits to museums, galleries, laboratories, agencies, businesses, stores, and organizations.

2. Observations of people, places, events, and nature.

3. Simulations through role plays, discussions, and games.

4. Attendance of meetings, conferences, and performances.

5. Field experiences in which one performs experiments or surveys.

6. Examinations of maps, charts, tables, graphs, collections, pictures, photographs, drawings, and models.

LOGICAL/MATHEMATICAL

You can find answers to many questions if you look in the right places. Sometimes these places are standard reference tools and sometimes these places are unusual reference aids. Think of one thing you could learn or find out if you looked at each of the following items:

- a thesaurus
- a biographical dictionary
- an atlas
- a cookbook
- an almanac
- a book of lists
- a telephone directory
- the yellow pages of a telephone directory
- the "S" volume of the encyclopedia
- a local newspaper
- a store directory
- a sales catalog

Using Multiple Resources to Find Answers

Page 2

VISUAL/SPATIAL

Create a poster that shows at least 25 different types of print materials that one might use as resources when researching a topic. Include traditional types of resources such as magazines and more unusual types of resources such as travel folders.

BODY/KINESTHETIC

Discuss situations in which an interview, survey, or hands-on experiment is the best way to find answers to questions when conducting research and writing reports.

MUSICAL/RHYTHMIC

Determine the research topics one might wish to pursue if your major reference tools were limited to records, album covers, top 20 songs on radio stations, concerts on television, musical films, videos about famous composers such as Mozart, and local symphonies and concerts.

INTERPERSONAL

Once a student has selected a topic to research and has located resources for information, he or she must decide on a format for sharing or reporting the results. Work with a friend to develop a large chart that shows at least 25 different products that could be used as possible formats. Consider such traditional products as posters and puppet shows, but also consider novel products such as learning kits and court trials.

INTRAPERSONAL

Evaluate your own strengths and weaknesses as a researcher and as a creator of writing projects.

Writing/Technology

Word Processor Wisdom

 ### VERBAL/LINGUISTIC
Using your own words, explain the purpose and multiple uses of a word processor in the area of writing.

 ### LOGICAL/MATHEMATICAL
Develop a flow chart or diagram to show how to use a word processor when completing various types of writing.

 ### VISUAL/SPATIAL
Design a billboard for your school grounds promoting the use of word processors in the teaching of writing at the middle school level. Make your billboard informative, interesting, colorful, and persuasive.

 ### BODY/KINESTHETIC
Use a piece of software to write an original short story, poem, essay, or report on a topic of your choice.

 ### MUSICAL/RHYTHMIC
Create a musical jingle promoting the use of word processors in the home and in the school.

 ### INTERPERSONAL
Working with a small group of peers, visit a computer store to examine the many different types of software available for improving the reading and writing skills of students. Prepare a mini-catalog or flyer describing each piece of software and rating its application in the classroom.

 ### INTRAPERSONAL
Decide whether you do your best creative writing sitting down with a pad of paper and a pencil or sitting at the computer using a special piece of software. Write down your feelings about or reactions to each of these very different approaches to writing.

Proverbs

Proverbs Are Wise Sayings

VERBAL/LINGUISTIC
A proverb is a short, wise saying that states a truth. Some examples of proverbs are:

The only way to have a friend is to be one.
A bird in hand is worth two in the bush.
He who hesitates is lost.

Locate ten different proverbs and write them down. Use one of them as the title of an original short story.

LOGICAL/MATHEMATICAL
Develop a set of logical arguments that (1) justify the need for proverbs that are handed down from generation to generation and that (2) document how selected proverbs evolved from historical events and experiences.

VISUAL/SPATIAL
Paint a mural with a theme that centers around various proverbs and their meanings.

BODY/KINESTHETIC
Write and perform a variety of scenarios or skits, each of which uses a different proverb as the outcome, punch line, or concluding statement.

MUSICAL/RHYTHMIC
Write down several interesting proverbs. For each proverb, select a different musical instrument that you best identify with its meaning. Justify your choices.

INTERPERSONAL
Work with a partner to rewrite ten favorite proverbs, substituting more sophisticated and lengthy words for those in the original saying. For example, one might rewrite the proverb **"He who hesitates is lost"** as **"A person of the masculine gender who falters when taking action is irreclaimable."** A thesaurus will be of great help in completing this task.

INTRAPERSONAL
Describe yourself, using at least five different proverbs to tell about your personality, habits, and/or values.

Creative Communications

Creative Writing, Thinking, and Speaking

VERBAL/LINGUISTIC
Write your own definition of creativity. Explain how a person can recognize a creative idea in his or her writing, thinking, or speaking.

LOGICAL/MATHEMATICAL
Think about the most creative people you know in your class or in your school. What special traits do these people demonstrate in writing, thinking, and/or speaking?

VISUAL/SPATIAL
Draw a picture or diagram that shows your ideas about what creativity is and is not.

BODY/KINESTHETIC
Write an original poem, skit, short story, tall tale, myth, fairy tale, or legend. Act out your words through creative dramatics.

MUSICAL/RHYTHMIC
Enhance your original writing in the Body/Kinesthetic activity with appropriate sounds or rhythms.

INTERPERSONAL
Plan and conduct a panel discussion on the topic of creativity in the classroom. Identify the types of classroom climate, assignments, tasks, tools, and resources that promote or inhibit creative acts by students. Discuss whether creativity is inherited and innate or whether it can be taught and nurtured.

INTRAPERSONAL
Rate your personal ability to write, think, and speak creatively when given classroom assignments, using a 1 to 10 scale. Consider 1 as "very low in creativity," 5 as "somewhat creative," and 10 as "highly creative." Give reasons for your rating decisions.

Listening Skills

The Payoffs of Active Listening

VERBAL/LINGUISTIC

Relate an anecdote of a time when someone really listened to what you were saying and this had a positive outcome. Tell about another time when someone did not listen to you, causing a real problem.

LOGICAL/MATHEMATICAL

Create a checklist of "Do I?" questions that someone could use to determine if he or she is a good listener. Two "Do I?" questions to get you started are:

1. **Do I look at a speaker when he or she is talking to me?**
2. **Do I ask questions when I don't understand something?**

VISUAL/SPATIAL

Create a cartoon or comic strip that shows good and bad listening habits.

BODY/KINESTHETIC

Act out a series of scenarios that demonstrate the barriers to good listening that commonly occur in personal conversations and discussions.

MUSICAL/RHYTHMIC

Experiment with the effects of different kinds of music on one's ability to listen and concentrate when conversing with someone else. What types of music encourage good listening skills and what types of music inhibit good listening skills?

INTERPERSONAL

Work with a small group of peers to develop a series of listening exercises that test one's ability to practice good active listening skills. Administer these exercises to members of the class and record your results.

INTRAPERSONAL

Write down what the following individuals would say about your ability to listen well:

1. your teacher
2. your parents
3. your friends

Using Learning Stations as an Instructional Tool

Learning stations come in every size, shape, and color, and can be placed in ordinary or unusual locations. A learning station can be as simple as a bulletin board station that is used by students for extra credit when their regular work is done, or as sophisticated as a series of technology stations around which the entire classroom program is organized. Learning stations can be used for teaching content or practicing skills on a daily basis, weekly basis, monthly basis, or for an entire semester.

The principal importance of a learning station is that it is a physical area where students engage in a variety of learning activities. An effective learning station (1) includes multilevel tasks; (2) offers choices in and alternatives to the tasks it requires; (3) is attractive and motivational; (4) provides clear directions and procedures; (5) accommodates three to five students at one sitting; (6) has flexible time limitations for completion; (7) controls and coordinates movement to and from or between stations; (8) incorporates varied learning styles, modalities, and intelligences; (9) manages student participation through recordkeeping strategies; and (10) encourages authentic types of assessment through the use of products and portfolios.

Some of the best formats for learning stations are:

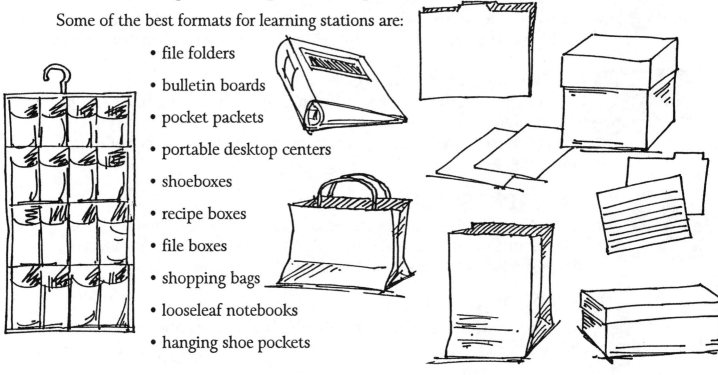

- file folders
- bulletin boards
- pocket packets
- portable desktop centers
- shoeboxes
- recipe boxes
- file boxes
- shopping bags
- looseleaf notebooks
- hanging shoe pockets

For more examples and explanations of learning station formats, see *Interdisciplinary Units and Projects for Thematic Instruction* by Imogene Forte and Sandra Schurr, Incentive Publications, 1995.

Some of the most practical ways to use space when setting up learning stations are the following:

Arrange desks in clusters of four or six.

Place an easel between two desks (or place two desks on each side of the easel).

Use bulletin boards or hanging displays in strategic positions.

Use round tables.

Place bookcases at an angle in a corner of the
room, adjacent to clustered desks or round tables.

Use backs of bookcases, teacher's desk, or other large pieces of furniture.

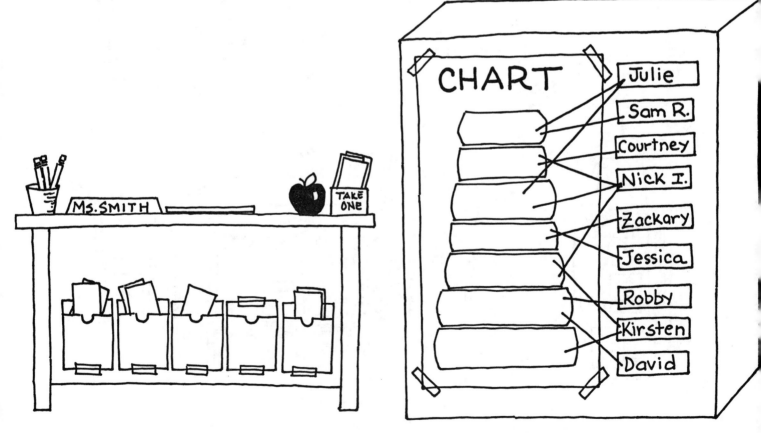

Arrange lap boards made of masonite or plywood around a carpeted area where students can sit on the floor.

Some evaluative techniques for use with learning stations that could become products and artifacts for a portfolio are:

- anecdotal records
- games, quizzes, puzzles
- logs and diaries
- teacher- or student-made tests
- class or individual charts, graphs
- checklists
- tape recordings
- suggestion boxes

- scrapbooks or notebooks
- observation records
- interviews
- conferences
- student rating scales
- daily progress reports
- library pockets with individual reporting cards

Finally, here are some things that should be considered before setting up learning stations in the middle level classroom:

1 Decide what you want to teach at each station. Write one or more student objectives. These should be things the student should do in order to show that he or she understands the concept or skill presented.

2 Decide on optional strategies, activities, and tasks for teaching those objectives.

3 Locate all supporting tools and materials for completing the assigned and/or optional tasks. Be sure that students know which materials are included in the station, how to use the materials, and how to care for them.

4 Write specific directions, procedures, and explanations for doing the work at the station. Give students an estimated timetable for completion of the station.

5 Plan for "traffic flow" in relation to other activities that will take place while the station is in use. Plan also for scheduling students into use of the stations. There are many ways to do this. Students can be scheduled to attend each station on a specific rotation. Provided there is room at a new station, students can move on to that station when they are finished with an assigned station. If the stations or station tasks are flexible and portable, students can take them to their seats. Finally, students can sign up for stations based on their interests and/or learning needs.

6 Introduce all station themes or names and the character and major content of each station before students actually begin tackling station activities. Be specific when you tell students what your expectations are in terms of their performance or achievement at each station, and be sure students understand how their achievements will be assessed. As part of this process, provide checkpoints where students may go for help should they forget or misunderstand initial instructions, or where students may review the information presented in this introduction.

Using Integrated Instructional Strategies to Develop Problem-solving and Higher-order Thinking Skills

USING BLOOM'S TAXONOMY
AS AN INSTRUCTIONAL TOOL
Overview 30
Activity Pages 32
USING WILLIAMS' TAXONOMY
AS AN INSTRUCTIONAL TOOL
Overview 42
Activity Pages 44
USING INVESTIGATION CARDS
AS AN INSTRUCTIONAL TOOL
Overview 50
Investigation Cards 51
USING CALENDARS AS
AN INSTRUCTIONAL TOOL
Overview 67
Calendars 69

Using Bloom's Taxonomy as an Instructional Tool

Bloom's Taxonomy is a well-known model for teaching critical thinking skills in any subject area. Based on the work of Benjamin Bloom, the taxonomy consists of six different thinking levels arranged in a hierarchy of difficulty.

Any student can function at each level of the taxonomy provided the content is appropriate for his or her reading ability. In order for teachers to consistently design lesson plans that incorporate all six levels, they should use the taxonomy to structure all student objectives, all information sessions, all questions, all assigned tasks, and all items on tests.

On the opposite page is a brief summary of the six taxonomy levels with a list of common student behaviors, presented as action verbs, associated with each level. When developing learning tasks and activities around Bloom's Taxonomy, it is important to include in each set at least one activity for each level of the taxonomy. Keep a copy of the Bloom's page in your lesson planning book so it will be handy when you need it.

Bloom's Taxonomy can be used to structure sets of learning tasks, student worksheets, cooperative learning group assignments, and independent study units. On the following pages you will find a collection of learning assignments based on this taxonomy. Topics were selected to be appealing to students and to fit into a middle grades curriculum.

Bloom's Taxonomy of Critical Thought

KNOWLEDGE LEVEL: Learn the information.

Sample Verbs: Define, find, follow directions, identify, know, label, list, memorize, name, quote, read, recall, recite, recognize, select, state, write.

COMPREHENSION LEVEL: Understand the information.

Sample Verbs: Account for, explain, express in other terms, give examples, give in own words, group, illustrate, infer, interpret, paraphrase, recognize, retell, show, simplify, summarize, translate.

APPLICATION LEVEL: Use the information.

Sample Verbs: Apply, compute, construct, construct using, convert (in math), demonstrate, derive, develop, discuss, generalize, interview, investigate, keep records, model, participate, perform, plan, produce, prove (in math), solve, use, utilize.

ANALYSIS LEVEL: Break the information down into its component parts.

Sample Verbs: Analyze, compare, contrast, criticize, debate, determine, diagram, differentiate, discover, draw conclusions, examine, infer, relate, search, sort, survey, take apart, uncover.

SYNTHESIS LEVEL: Put information together in new and different ways.

Sample Verbs: Build, combine, create, design, imagine, invent, make up, present, produce, propose.

EVALUATION LEVEL: Judge the information.

Sample Verbs: Assess, defend, evaluate, grade, judge, measure, perform a critique, rank, recommend, select, test, validate, verify.

Parts of Speech

Verb Review

KNOWLEDGE

Define the word **verb**.

COMPREHENSION

Draw three different pictures to illustrate the sentence below using each of these three verbs:

screamed   clapped   ran

When the bell rang, everyone jumped up and _____.

APPLICATION

Write a journal entry or page for your diary about an interesting experience you have shared with a classmate recently. Underline all the verbs used. Ask the classmate to do the same thing at the same time. Comparing the completed assignments and the verb usage will be fun and should definitely show you how much difference the choice of verbs used in writing can make.

SYNTHESIS

Design a special study aid for people learning to use English as a second language. Give rules for using nouns, verbs, adverbs, and adjectives. Give examples as well.

ANALYSIS

Compare and contrast verbs and adverbs and their uses. Use a Venn diagram to show your findings.

EVALUATION

Devise an authentic assessment product or performance task to evaluate your own understanding of and use of verbs.

Poetry

Poetry Pickup

KNOWLEDGE

Define **metaphor**, **haiku**, **tonka**, **cinquain**, and **limerick**.

COMPREHENSION

Construct a poetry book of your own. Include selected poems that you enjoy from anthologies of your choice. Copy the poems in your best handwriting, illustrate them, and fasten the pages together to make a book.

APPLICATION

Select a poem from your collection to read aloud to a friend. Practice reading the poem before asking the friend to listen to you and rate your oral reading skills according to the following criteria:
. . . **use of expression**
. . . **voice projection**
. . . **gestures**
. . . **attention holders**

SYNTHESIS

Outline a lesson plan to use to encourage students in grade three, four, or five to write poetry. Specify grade level, form of poetry, and sequence of steps.

ANALYSIS

Compare and contrast the characteristics of three forms of poetry: **tonka**, **cinquain**, and **haiku**.

EVALUATION

Select a form of poetry to use to write a poem about yourself. Share the poem with your classmates. Then participate in a total group discussion to present a critique of each poem.

Journalism

News and Views

KNOWLEDGE

Quickly skim a daily newspaper. Make a list of the important components of the newspaper. Check the articles that you want to come back to and read more carefully.

ANALYSIS

Read the "letters to the editor" page and select three of the letters with which to either agree or disagree. Justify your positions.

SYNTHESIS

Write a letter to the editor stating your views on a topic about which you have strong feelings. Reread your letter carefully. Determine if you have stated an objective case for your cause or if it reflects a personal bias.

COMPREHENSION

Read the paper in detail giving particular attention to the writing styles, accuracy, and interest of various parts of the paper.

EVALUATION

Prepare a plan for a class newspaper with articles that will be beneficial and of high interest to all members of the class.

APPLICATION

Use the paper to locate information related to upcoming events (i.e., movies, exhibits, fairs, etc.) that you might want to attend.

Test Taking

A Takeoff on Tests

KNOWLEDGE

Using your own words, write definitions of the following types of tests: **intelligence tests, achievement tests,** and **aptitude tests.**

ANALYSIS

Examine the test items on a standardized achievement test. Classify these items in as many ways as you can.

COMPREHENSION

Explain the major purpose of each type of test (**intelligence, achievement,** and **aptitude**). For each one, give an example of a situation in which that particular test would be the most appropriate one to use.

SYNTHESIS

Devise three word problems appropriate for use as test items on an achievement test for students in your age group. Solve the problems and determine if they would be easy, difficult, or very difficult for others to solve.

APPLICATION

Examine samples of intelligence tests, achievement tests, and aptitude tests. Design a survey to determine the effectiveness of each. Administer the survey to ten of your classmates and show the survey results to others in the class.

EVALUATION

Determine the most appropriate test for each of the following :
- **student class placement**
- **career counseling**
- **after-school tutorials**
- **individualized instruction**
- **summer enrichment programs** (i.e., **music, art, speech, etc.**)

Storytelling
Storytelling

KNOWLEDGE

Brainstorm a list of all the different types of stories that you remember from childhood, your reading, and your studies in school (tall tales, legends, myths, etc.).

ANALYSIS

Consult anthologies and other reference materials to learn about storytellers and the role of stories in different countries and cultures. Read a collection of stories portraying one particular setting or perspective. Develop a criteria for determining the effectiveness of the storyteller's efforts to motivate the listener or reader to develop sympathy for the cause or concerns portrayed in the stories.

COMPREHENSION

Explain how storytelling has been used through the ages to both shape a culture in its formative stages and to record the history of the culture for future generations.

SYNTHESIS

Create a song or skit or develop a series of illustrations to accompany a story by one of your favorite storytellers. Try to reflect the storyteller's mood or special style with your work.

APPLICATION

Make a collection of stories to share with your family or with a group of friends. Decide on the setting in which the stories will be enjoyed (bedtime, around a campfire, during class, etc.) and select stories appropriate for the setting.

EVALUATION

Write an original story based on a personal experience. Reflecting on what you have learned about storytellers and their stories through the ages, try to make your story as interesting as possible, while at the same time giving an account of the event as it actually happened.

Editing Process

Editor's Guidelines

KNOWLEDGE

Make a list of as many rules as you can think of that editors should follow.

COMPREHENSION

Review your list of editors' rules and develop a "top ten" list of the most important ones.

APPLICATION

Use your top ten list of editors' rules to edit a piece of original writing. Determine the effectiveness of your list by the ease and efficiency of its use and the quality of your completed writing.

ANALYSIS

Select an article, an essay, or a chapter from your science or social studies text. Using your top ten rules for editing, assess the quality of editing of the work. Rate the editor's contribution to the work on a scale of 1 to 5.

SYNTHESIS

Devise a quick and easy checklist to be used by students of your age in editing written assignments in math, science, and social studies.

EVALUATION

Determine the importance of each of the following in the editorial process:

- **using proofreading marks**
- **conveying author's purpose**
- **summarizing information**
- **deleting irrelevant or unrelated matter**
- **adding interest through figures of speech, forceful repetition, and declarative expressions**
- **establishing sequence of events, clarity of thought, and sustained writing style**
- **careful attention to punctuation, spelling, and grammar**

Biography/Autobiography

A View of You

COMPREHENSION

Explain the main differences between using a biography to make a record of a person's life for future generations and using an autobiography for the same purpose.

APPLICATION

Use reference materials from the library to examine examples of both a biography and an autobiography of a selected historical figure. Make notes on both the mood and factual accounts of the two volumes. Summarize your notes to reflect the similarities and differences portrayed by the two authors.

KNOWLEDGE

Using your own words, write a definition of a biography and one of an autobiography.

A View of You

ANALYSIS

Using the notes and summary acquired from examining the biography and autobiography of the selected historical figure, determine which was the most interesting account of the person's life and which left the most favorable impression of the subject's personality and/or contribution to the world in which he or she lived.

SYNTHESIS

Use the accompanying "personal information survey" to summarize information about your own life to date. Use the information to write a brief but concise autobiography.

Ask a friend to use the same "personal information survey" to gather information to write your biography.

EVALUATION

Examine the completed autobiography and the completed biography to find out how your own "view of you" compares with another writer's view.

Note: You will, of course, want to exchange favors with your biographer by following the same procedures to produce a biography and autobiography of him or her. The conversation following the writing exercises should be lively and informative, especially if both parties have attempted to be as objective as possible.

A View of You

PERSONAL INFORMATION SURVEY

Interview date_____

Person's full name _____

Time of person's life_____

Place of birth _____

Places lived during lifetime

_____   _____

_____   _____

Person's early life (parents, home, school, significant events)
Person's later life (goals, achievements, other items of note)
Important personal interests or distinguishing characteristics
Brief summary of the person's life, accomplishments, and distinctions

Literature

For Fiction's Sake

KNOWLEDGE

After a lot of deliberation, select a book of fiction that has special appeal for you. Read and enjoy the book.

COMPREHENSION

Review the book's main points and major happenings. Make notes to enable you to construct a time line or flow chart to summarize the plot and sequence of events.

APPLICATION

Make a list of new words, descriptive phrases, or memorable visual images that you encountered in the book. Think about how the author's writing style and word usage may influence or enhance your appreciation for the written word.

ANALYSIS

Write a review of the book for a local paper. Try to give a true picture of your "feel" for the book and its author. Also, as a good reviewer, try to objectively pinpoint both strengths and weaknesses of the work.

SYNTHESIS

Write a letter that one of the main characters in the book might have written to another one of the characters—after the story was over!

EVALUATION

Determine the author's point of view and evaluate how effective he or she was in transmitting that point of view to the reader.

Using Williams' Taxonomy as an Instructional Tool

Williams' Taxonomy is another important model to use when teaching thinking skills. While Bloom's Taxonomy is used for teaching critical thinking skills, Williams' Taxonomy is used for teaching creative thinking skills.

Although there is a relationship between these two models, and even some overlap, it should be noted that critical thinking tends to be more reactive and vertical in nature while creative thinking tends to be more proactive and lateral in nature. Another way of saying this is that critical thinking tends to involve tasks that are logical, rational, sequential, analytical, and convergent. Creative thinking, on the other hand, tends to involve tasks that are spatial, flexible, spontaneous, analogical, and divergent. Critical thinking is "left brain" thinking while creative thinking is "right brain" thinking.

Williams' Taxonomy has eight levels, also arranged in a hierarchy, with certain types of student behavior associated with each level. The first four levels of the Williams' model are cognitive in nature while the last four levels are affective in nature.

It is strongly suggested that a teacher keep a copy of Williams' Taxonomy in the lesson plan book so that the levels and behaviors can be an integral part of most lesson plans and student assignments. On the opposite page is a brief overview of the levels in Williams' Taxonomy. Each level is accompanied by a few cue words to be used to trigger student responses to a given creative stimulus or challenge.

The following pages offer a wide variety of student worksheets, assignments, independent study guides, or group problem-solving tasks, covering many different content areas appropriate for middle grade classrooms.

Williams' Taxonomy of Creative Thought

FLUENCY

Enables the learner to generate a great many ideas, related answers, or choices in a given situation.

Sample Cue Words: Generating oodles, lots, many ideas.

FLEXIBILITY

Lets the learner change everyday objects to generate a variety of categories by taking detours and varying sizes, shapes, quantities, time limits, requirements, objectives, or dimensions in a given situation.

Sample Cue Words: Generating varied, different, alternative ideas.

ORIGINALITY

Causes the learner to seek new ideas by suggesting unusual twists to change content or by coming up with clever responses to a given situation.

Sample Cue Words: Generating unusual, unique, new ideas.

ELABORATION

Helps the learner stretch by expanding, enlarging, enriching, or embellishing possibilities that build on previous thoughts or ideas.

Sample Cue Words: Generating enriched, embellished, expanded ideas.

RISK TAKING

Enables the learner to deal with the unknown by taking chances, experimenting with new ideas, or trying new challenges.

Sample Cue Words: Experimenting with and exploring ideas.

COMPLEXITY

Permits the learner to create structure in an unstructured setting or to build a logical order in a given situation.

Sample Cue Words: Improving and explaining ideas.

CURIOSITY

Encourages the learner to follow a hunch, question alternatives, ponder outcomes, and wonder about options in a given situation.

Sample Cue Words: Pondering and questioning ideas.

IMAGINATION

Allows the learner to visualize possibilities, build images in his or her mind, picture new objects, or reach beyond the limits of the practical.

Sample Cue Words: Visualizing and fantasizing ideas.

Language Arts

Pasta Perfect

FLUENCY

List as many types of pasta as you can.

FLEXIBILITY

Think of twenty ways to prepare and serve different forms of pasta. Group your list of forms in some meaningful way.

ORIGINALITY

According to mythology, pasta was introduced to Italy by Marco Polo after a visit to China in 1271. Historians, however, say pasta was already a staple of many Italian kitchens well before that date. Create a clever skit or play to tell about the origin and history of pasta as a food of the world. Select a cast of characters for your skit (classmates) and present the skit to your class.

ELABORATION

Agree or disagree with this statement and expound on your decision:

Pasta contains more food value than does rice, and contributes more to a healthy diet.

44

Pasta Perfect

Page 2

RISK TAKING
Take a position on whether pasta or pizza should be
served for your school cafeteria's Friday lunch selection
(salad, drinks, and dessert will remain the same in both
instances). Outline a plan to convince your classmates to
think as you do.

COMPLEXITY
Discuss ways the taste, texture, and nutritious value of
commercially dried pasta and home-rolled fresh pasta differ.

CURIOSITY
Make a list of things consumers need to know about the
manufacturing, packaging, and marketing of commercially
distributed pasta sauces.

IMAGINATION
Visualize, describe, and draw a series of three sketches to
show a brand new type of pasta, the packaging including a
description on the container, and a recipe for its use.

Listening Skills

Listening In

FLUENCY
Make a list of all the different situations in which you might want to listen to other people's conversations.

FLEXIBILITY
List several careers that depend on the effective use of listening skills.

ORIGINALITY
Determine the two most interesting places in your community for "listening in" on conversations between two or more speakers. Describe the two settings and use a columned chart to diagram similarities of and differences between the types of conversation one would hear in the two places.

ELABORATION
What are the differences in the following?
- two people gossiping
- reporting
- accounting
- elaborating on a given set of circumstances

RISK TAKING
Draw a cartoon or comic strip showing a time that you remember being glad that no one was around to listen to and report on something you said.

Listening In

COMPLEXITY

Explain the significance of one or both of these statements:

"Sticks and stones may break my bones, but words will never harm me."

"Actions speak louder than words."

CURIOSITY

Generate a collection of questions related to attentive listening, analytical listening, appreciative listening, and marginal listening skills that you would want to ask each of the following people:

- an orchestra conductor
- a private detective
- a gossip columnist
- a middle grade teacher
- a wildlife photographer

IMAGINATION

Visualize yourself as the script writer and producer of a soon-to-be-aired television mini-series. The main character is a senior citizen whose retirement hobby is finding and recognizing teenagers in the act of bringing good cheer to an underprivileged person. Outline the script for your first show and give examples of how listening skills would play an important part in the plot.

Reference Materials

Reference Referral

 ## FLUENCY
Write a paragraph on the topic of using reference materials as a tool for student success. Tell why they are necessary, where they can be located, and the penalties paid for carelessness in their use.

 ## FLEXIBILITY
Create a poster illustrating as many types of reference materials as you can think of which are available to students in your school.

 ## ORIGINALITY
Some common forms of reference materials found in most school libraries are encyclopedias, world almanacs, dictionaries, thesauruses, magazines, and newspapers. List each of these reference tools on a sheet of paper and try to give at least one way each one could be used in an unusual manner to aid students in your school to develop more original and/or creative content-based reports or projects.

 ## ELABORATION
Elaborate on this statement: **"You will find it a very good practice always to verify your references, sir."**—Martin Joseph Routh

 ## RISK TAKING
Write a position paper, to discuss in a total group setting, on "using reference materials to promote cooperative learning and group interaction as opposed to the traditional independent research paper."

 ## COMPLEXITY
Devise a skit to demonstrate ways reference materials have been abused or overused by teachers and students in the traditional test-centered classrooms.

 ## CURIOSITY
Select a math, social studies, or science topic that you would like to (or need to) know more about. Use the attached "Guide for a Content Area Report or Project," to develop a lesson plan complete with time table and list of questions to answer. List the reference materials you will need to complete the study.

 ## IMAGINATION
Imagine what the world would be like if there were no written or recorded reference materials, and everyone had to rely on oral communication and imagination.

Reference Materials

GUIDE FOR DEVELOPING A CONTENT AREA REPORT OR PROJECT

Name _____

Topic _____

Type of report or project _____

Date to begin _____ Date to finish _____

QUESTIONS TO FIND ANSWERS FOR
REFERENCES NEEDED
STUDY PLAN

Using Investigation Cards as an Instructional Tool

Investigation Cards provide a tool for differentiating instruction in a classroom of diverse abilities, interests, and cultures. The cards are designed around Bloom's Taxonomy of Cognitive Development, with three tasks written for each of the six levels. This makes Investigation Cards helpful in "smuggling thinking skills into the curriculum."

Investigation Cards can be used in several ways. Teachers can assign cards to students, or students can select their own cards. Teachers can require students to complete at least one card at each level of the taxonomy, or they can require students to complete cards at any given level or levels of the taxonomy. Teachers can also assign Investigation Cards to cooperative learning groups, with each group having the same set of cards, or each group working on a different set. Finally, Investigation Cards make excellent homework assignments, enrichment assignments, or assignments for students with special needs.

You will need a supply of blank 4" x 6" file cards to prepare the Investigation Cards. Make three copies of each page of graphic cards in this book. Cut apart the cards on the dotted lines and paste each one on the back of one of the 4" x 6" file cards. Then make a copy of each page of task cards, cut apart the cards on the dotted lines, and paste each task card on the back of the appropriate graphic card. If time permits, color the graphics and laminate the set of Investigation Cards for extended use. If time is limited, you may make copies of the task cards alone, cut them apart, and give each student or group of students the paper task cards for immediate use.

Students and teachers can make additional sets of Investigation Cards on topics of their choice by following these simple steps:

1 Select an object or topic of interest to you in your subject area that lends itself to the Investigation Card concept.

2 Collect information associated with your object or topic and use this information to identify major terms, background data, or major concepts related to your Investigation Card theme.

3 Write three different questions, tasks, challenges, or activities for each level of Bloom's Taxonomy, using the object or topic as the springboard for ideas. The Bloom Cue Charts found in three Incentive Publications books—*The Definitive Middle School Guide; Tools, Treasures, and Measures;* and *Science Mind Stretchers*—offer excellent guidance for this purpose.

LANGUAGE ARTS

Investigate the
Magic of Language

GRAPHIC CARD

LANGUAGE ARTS

Investigate the
Magic of Language

GRAPHIC CARD

LANGUAGE ARTS

Investigate the
Magic of Language

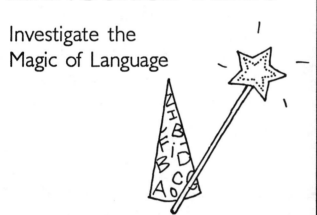

GRAPHIC CARD

LANGUAGE ARTS

Investigate the
Magic of Language

GRAPHIC CARD

LANGUAGE ARTS

Investigate the
Magic of Language

GRAPHIC CARD

LANGUAGE ARTS

Investigate the
Magic of Language

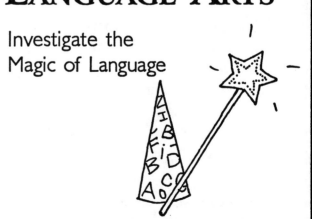

GRAPHIC CARD

KNOWLEDGE

Define these concepts: **homonym, synonym, homophone,** and **antonym.** Write four sentences to illustrate these concepts. Underline the pertinent words in each sentence. (For example, underline the two words that are homonyms in the "homonym sentence."

TASK CARD

Investigate the Magic of Language

COMPREHENSION

Describe your "favorite word" in the English language.

TASK CARD

Investigate the Magic of Language

KNOWLEDGE

Define these terms: **noun, pronoun, verb, adjective, adverb, preposition, conjunction, article,** and **interjection.** Find an example of each in the local newspaper.

TASK CARD

Investigate the Magic of Language

COMPREHENSION

Etymology is the study of the origin of words. Choose a word from the dictionary and explain how you think this word came to mean what it does now.

TASK CARD

Investigate the Magic of Language

KNOWLEDGE

Define these terms: **pun, personification, simile, idiom, onomatopoeia, hyperbole, alliteration,** and **metaphor.** Record an example of each from your English textbook or a book of literature.

TASK CARD

Investigate the Magic of Language

COMPREHENSION

Think of a word that creates a powerful image in your mind. Summarize your reaction to this word using the five senses. When you say the word, what do you see, hear, smell, taste, and feel?

TASK CARD

Investigate the Magic of Language

APPLICATION

Locate one magazine illustration or newspaper photograph to illustrate each of these figures of speech: **pun, personification, simile, idiom, onomatopoeia, hyperbole, alliteration,** and **metaphor.** Write a sentence to accompany each one.

TASK CARD

Investigate the Magic of Language

ANALYSIS

Debate which of the following sentence beginnings is easiest and most fun for you and your peers to write:

a. a sentence that begins with an adverb
b. a sentence that begins with a prepositional phrase
c. a sentence that begins with an adjective
d. a sentence that begins with a present or past participle

TASK CARD

Investigate the Magic of Language

APPLICATION

Locate a magazine advertisement. Rewrite the advertising message, substituting synonyms, homonyms, antonyms, and homophones wherever possible. Notice how these changes affect the impact of the ad.

TASK CARD

Investigate the Magic of Language

ANALYSIS

Determine what would be a *better* word to substitute for each of the following "very" phrases:

a. very stupid   **f.** very pretty
b. very far   **g.** very weak
c. very near   **h.** very small
d. very large   **i.** very strong
e. very hot   **j.** very quiet

TASK CARD

Investigate the Magic of Language

APPLICATION

Locate various comic strips in the newspaper and study them. Then use a comic strip format to prepare a series of frames on the topic of grammar and parts of speech. First write a definition of each part of speech. Then write a series of related sentences illustrating each part of speech, using humor in your message. Draw pictures, cartoon style, to illustrate each sentence.

TASK CARD

Investigate the Magic of Language

ANALYSIS

Deduce which of the following would be more difficult and frustrating for you and your peers to write:

- a nine-word sentence in which each odd-numbered word is the word "now"
- a nine-word sentence in which each even-numbered word is the word "now"

TASK CARD

Investigate the Magic of Language

SYNTHESIS

Create an original word puzzle by providing definitions of words that will form a pyramid. Each new level of the pyramid should be formed by letters the same as the level below, but with one fewer letter. *Example:*

nineteenth letter of the alphabet	S
similar to	A S
sugar from a tree	S A P
as soon as possible	A S A P
spaghetti	P A S T A

TASK CARD

Investigate the Magic of Language

EVALUATION

Select five poems that you like, each by a different poet. Order them from 1 to 5, with 1 being the poem richest in the use of figurative language and 5 being the poem most lacking in figurative language. Be able to defend your choices.

TASK CARD

Investigate the Magic of Language

SYNTHESIS

Word associations can be lots of fun. Write down any starter word and a totally unrelated ending word. Then choose three words to go in between the two words to relate each to the next in some logical way.

***Example:* WORM and CURIOUS**

WORM → earth → planets → scientist → CURIOUS

TASK CARD

Investigate the Magic of Language

EVALUATION

Justify the use of word processors as part of the schooling process in today's classrooms.

TASK CARD

Investigate the Magic of Language

SYNTHESIS

Try writing a series of short poems using "opposite" words for the title. Sample titles and topics:

Disciplined Freedom
playing guitar
school
democracy
tennis

Pleasing Pain
a cold shower
getting a shot
being tickled
caring for a pet
removal of braces

Repulsive Attraction
a baby skunk
a cactus flower
a car accident
a roller coaster
a candy bar when on a diet

TASK CARD

Investigate the Magic of Language

EVALUATION

Prepare a critique of a set of your creative writing papers from the perspective of word choice and rich vocabulary. Are there places where you could improve the quality of your work by using synonyms, homonyms, homophones, or antonyms in appropriate places?

TASK CARD

Investigate the Magic of Language

LANGUAGE ARTS

Investigate the Alphabet

GRAPHIC CARD

LANGUAGE ARTS

Investigate the Alphabet

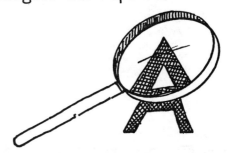

GRAPHIC CARD

LANGUAGE ARTS

Investigate the Alphabet

GRAPHIC CARD

LANGUAGE ARTS

Investigate the Alphabet

GRAPHIC CARD

LANGUAGE ARTS

Investigate the Alphabet

GRAPHIC CARD

LANGUAGE ARTS

Investigate the Alphabet

GRAPHIC CARD

KNOWLEDGE

Define **alphabet, vowels,** and **consonants.**

TASK CARD

Investigate the Alphabet

COMPREHENSION

Summarize the ways people communicated with one another before the development of the alphabet.

TASK CARD

Investigate the Alphabet

KNOWLEDGE

Reproduce the letters of the alphabet and write down an unusual and interesting word from the dictionary for each letter.

TASK CARD

Investigate the Alphabet

COMPREHENSION

Describe things people could not do before the invention of the alphabet.

TASK CARD

Investigate the Alphabet

KNOWLEDGE

Record one contribution of each of the following cultures to the development of the alphabet:
a.   the Egyptians
b.   the Semites
c.   the Phoenicians
d.   the Greeks
e.   the Romans

TASK CARD

Investigate the Alphabet

COMPREHENSION

Give a brief explanation and example of each of the following stages of early writing:
• ideography
• logography

TASK CARD

Investigate the Alphabet

APPLICATION

Practice writing a simple rebus story, report, or essay.

TASK CARD

Investigate the Alphabet

ANALYSIS

Examine the Braille alphabet and form a set of generalizations about its characters, organization, and usefulness.

TASK CARD

Investigate the Alphabet

APPLICATION

Locate the alphabet characters of at least one important language other than English, such as Greek, Hebrew, or Japanese. Write them down.

TASK CARD

Investigate the Alphabet

ANALYSIS

Examine the "sign language" system and form a set of generalizations about its characters, organization, and usefulness.

TASK CARD

Investigate the Alphabet

APPLICATION

Search through the picture book section of your local library or that of an elementary school library for examples of creative ABC books. Write down the titles, authors, and publishers of at least 5–10 books and a brief synopsis of each.

TASK CARD

Investigate the Alphabet

ANALYSIS

Examine the Morse Code system and form a set of generalizations about its characters, organization, and usefulness.

TASK CARD

Investigate the Alphabet

SYNTHESIS

Invent an original code or cipher and use it to send a series of secret messages to a friend. See if your friend can "crack the code" without your help.

TASK CARD

Investigate the Alphabet

EVALUATION

Argue for or against this statement: **"Everyone should learn to speak, read, and write a second language."**

TASK CARD

Investigate the Alphabet

SYNTHESIS

Create an original ABC book on a special theme that would appeal to a young child. Be sure to illustrate it.

TASK CARD

Investigate the Alphabet

EVALUATION

Engage in a debate over the importance of individual letters of the alphabet. What is the most important letter and what is the least important? Be able to defend your choices.

TASK CARD

Investigate the Alphabet

SYNTHESIS

Write an informative ABC report on an academic topic of your choice. Your report should have one important fact for each letter of the alphabet and should include graphics, charts, graphs, diagrams, or illustrations where appropriate.

TASK CARD

Investigate the Alphabet

EVALUATION

Agree or disagree with this statement: **"The English alphabet is not well suited to writing words in English because it does not have a separate character for every distinctive sound in English, and it has several characters with more than one sound."** Give examples to support your position.

TASK CARD

Investigate the Alphabet

LANGUAGE ARTS

Investigate a Book of Fiction

GRAPHIC CARD

LANGUAGE ARTS

Investigate a Book of Fiction

GRAPHIC CARD

LANGUAGE ARTS

Investigate a Book of Fiction

GRAPHIC CARD

LANGUAGE ARTS

Investigate a Book of Fiction

GRAPHIC CARD

LANGUAGE ARTS

Investigate a Book of Fiction

GRAPHIC CARD

LANGUAGE ARTS

Investigate a Book of Fiction

GRAPHIC CARD

KNOWLEDGE

List the **who, what, when,** and **where** of the story.

TASK CARD

Investigate a Book of Fiction

COMPREHENSION

Using only three words, describe the physical appearance of the main character in the story. Give examples from the story to support your word choices.

TASK CARD

Investigate a Book of Fiction

KNOWLEDGE

Record five major events from the story in chronological order.

TASK CARD

Investigate a Book of Fiction

COMPREHENSION

In your own words, briefly describe one special event, adventure, conflict, or episode that was important to the development of the story.

TASK CARD

Investigate a Book of Fiction

KNOWLEDGE

Select a passage from the story and practice reading it aloud to your classmates. Try to pick a descriptive passage that makes good use of figurative language.

TASK CARD

Investigate a Book of Fiction

COMPREHENSION

Illustrate the setting of the story with either a large drawing or a map.

TASK CARD

Investigate a Book of Fiction

APPLICATION

Locate five to ten words from the story that are unfamiliar to you. Look them up in a dictionary and write down the definition of each as it is used in the story.

©1996 Incentive Publications, Inc., Nashville, TN.

TASK CARD

Investigate a Book of Fiction

ANALYSIS

Differentiate the way the main character talks, acts, thinks, and behaves at the beginning of the story from the way he or she talks, acts, thinks, and behaves at the end of the story.

©1996 Incentive Publications, Inc., Nashville, TN.

TASK CARD

Investigate a Book of Fiction

APPLICATION

Record three facts and three opinions from the story.

©1996 Incentive Publications, Inc., Nashville, TN.

TASK CARD

Investigate a Book of Fiction

ANALYSIS

Compare and contrast any two characters in the story. Consider comparing the protagonist and the antagonist if the story has both. How are they alike and how are they different?

©1996 Incentive Publications, Inc., Nashville, TN.

TASK CARD

Investigate a Book of Fiction

APPLICATION

Locate ten different personal pronouns in the story such as **he, she, it, they, them, him,** or **her.** Write each one on a piece of paper along with the number of the page on which it was found and an indication of the paragraph. Next to each pronoun, write the name of the noun to which it refers.

©1996 Incentive Publications, Inc., Nashville, TN.

TASK CARD

Investigate a Book of Fiction

ANALYSIS

Examine one major passage from the story. Complete this statement: "**The main idea of this passage is . . .**"

©1996 Incentive Publications, Inc., Nashville, TN.

TASK CARD

Investigate a Book of Fiction

SYNTHESIS

Create a book jacket for your work of fiction. Make it colorful, informative, and interesting.

TASK CARD

Investigate a Book of Fiction

EVALUATION

Decide if the main character of this story would make a good friend or not. What criteria would you use to judge a good friend? How does this character measure up to your standards? Write a paragraph to justify your decision.

TASK CARD

Investigate a Book of Fiction

SYNTHESIS

Design a set of test questions that the teacher might choose to administer to someone who has read this story.

TASK CARD

Investigate a Book of Fiction

EVALUATION

Suppose you were to make three recommendations to the author and/or the publisher for improving this story. Describe your recommendations.

TASK CARD

Investigate a Book of Fiction

SYNTHESIS

Write a new, unusual, and different ending for the story— one with a twist.

TASK CARD

Investigate a Book of Fiction

EVALUATION

If you were to give this story a Book Award, which of the following would you offer and why?

Best Author
Best Fiction Story
Best Main Character
Best Supporting Character
Best Use of Descriptive Language
Best Illustration
Best Middle School Book
Best Use of Setting

TASK CARD

Investigate a Book of Fiction

Language Arts

Investigate a Dictionary

GRAPHIC CARD

Language Arts

Investigate a Dictionary

GRAPHIC CARD

Language Arts

Investigate a Dictionary

GRAPHIC CARD

Language Arts

Investigate a Dictionary

GRAPHIC CARD

Language Arts

Investigate a Dictionary

GRAPHIC CARD

Language Arts

Investigate a Dictionary

GRAPHIC CARD

KNOWLEDGE

List all the different types of information you can find in your dictionary.

TASK CARD

Investigate a Dictionary

COMPREHENSION

Describe how each of the following individuals is most likely to use a dictionary at work: media specialist, editor, teacher, journalist, secretary, and author.

TASK CARD

Investigate a Dictionary

KNOWLEDGE

Select any ten pages from the dictionary at random and write down the pairs of guide words that you find on each page. Record the page numbers of each pair of words.

TASK CARD

Investigate a Dictionary

COMPREHENSION

Explain the meaning of each of these words, then provide another name for each one: **courier, angler, buccaneer, mason, orator, crony,** and **mariner.**

TASK CARD

Investigate a Dictionary

KNOWLEDGE

Indicate ten situations in which you as a student found the dictionary useful. Be specific as you recall these events.

TASK CARD

Investigate a Dictionary

COMPREHENSION

Draw and color the following beach scene:

"Beside a dwelling of sand sits an umber mollusk. An ebony osprey soars overhead. In the azure sky is a cumulus formation. A cluster of palm trees in full foliage surrounds the east side of the beach. A young lady sits on a scarlet towel and devours a boysenberry ice cream treat."

TASK CARD

Investigate a Dictionary

APPLICATION

Use the dictionary to find the differences between an **alligator** and a **crocodile,** between a **spider** and a **grasshopper,** between a **moth** and a **butterfly,** and between an **eagle** and a **condor.**

　　　TASK CARD

Investigate a Dictionary

ANALYSIS

Choose three mystery words from the dictionary and write five clues to the meaning of one of them. Have a friend do the same. Exchange mystery words and analyze the clues to determine which word is being described.

　　　TASK CARD

Investigate a Dictionary

APPLICATION

Discover the meaning of each of the following words through use of a dictionary: **isosceles, monocle, akimbo, garret, festoon, siphon, impetigo, dormer,** and **cutlass.** Draw a picture to show the meaning of each word.

　　　TASK CARD

Investigate a Dictionary

ANALYSIS

Compare and contrast the dictionary with the thesaurus. How are they alike and how are they different?

　　　TASK CARD

Investigate a Dictionary

APPLICATION

Using the dictionary as an information source, determine what you would do with each of the following objects: **hyacinth, epaulet, landau, prawn, lentil, dredge, snood, howdah, jersey, smock, creel,** and **stenographer.**

　　　TASK CARD

Investigate a Dictionary

ANALYSIS

Examine the dictionary and draw conclusions about the types of words that we borrow from other cultures. Give examples to reflect your conclusions.

　　　TASK CARD

Investigate a Dictionary

SYNTHESIS

Invent a new word. Spell your word correctly and determine its part(s) of speech. Then divide your word into syllables and write a phonetic spelling. Use two or three sentences to tell what your word means.

TASK CARD

Investigate a Dictionary

EVALUATION

A dictionary gives us several types of information about a word. Order these information types according to their helpfulness to you. Give reasons for your first and last choices.

TASK CARD

Investigate a Dictionary

SYNTHESIS

Create a dictionary of terms for an unusual topic or theme such as **monsters, superstars, mystery buffs, magicians, detectives, serpents,** or **geniuses.**

TASK CARD

Investigate a Dictionary

EVALUATION

If you were to give an award for the most versatile reference source from the following list, which one would you choose? Give reasons for your answer.

- thesaurus
- dictionary
- atlas
- almanac
- encyclopedia

TASK CARD

Investigate a Dictionary

SYNTHESIS

Design a magazine ad for the world's first "talking dictionary." What propaganda technique will you use?

TASK CARD

Investigate a Dictionary

EVALUATION

An idiom is a word combination that has a special meaning. It is often listed in a dictionary under the most important word in the phrase. The idiom is usually printed in small, dark type, and is found after the definition of the entry word. Which idiom best describes you at this moment? Explain.

see eye to eye   **take heart**
off the record   **hit it off**
nip and tuck   **duck's soup**

TASK CARD

Investigate a Dictionary

Using Calendars as an Instructional Tool

Contemporary calendars come in all colors, shapes, and sizes. They cover a wide range of themes and messages, often providing the user with much information for thought and motivation for action. A calendar is considered by many to be an art form and a teaching tool as well as a time management aid. Visit a book store, a gift shop, or the card section of a drug store and you will find calendars for everyone from "cat owners" and "movie buffs" to "Snoopy fans" and "nature lovers." Museums often carry calendars on educational topics.

The calendars on the following pages were designed to be used as mini-interdisciplinary units. The activities were chosen to:

- develop skills;
- introduce new concepts;
- stimulate curiosity; and
- present challenges.

These calendar tasks can be used as:

- enrichment;
- homework;
- extra credit assignments; or
- an addition to the traditional curriculum.

A wide variety of instructional springboards are included for each day of a typical month. Students can:

- complete each day's task as given;
- select one task to complete each week;
- be assigned a particular set of tasks by the teacher; or
- complete the tasks collaboratively with a group of peers.

67

One way to introduce the use of calendars as an instructional tool in the classroom is to have students bring in favorite calendars from home or solicit discarded calendars from retail outlets. Display these calendars and use them as the basis for group discussions and/or student observations. Some starter questions or tasks might be:

1 Who would buy this calendar and why?

2 What could one learn by using this calendar?

3 How are graphics, color, layout, and design used to enhance the theme and appeal of this calendar?

4 Why is a calendar considered by some people to be a "form of modern art"?

5 Why would someone want to collect calendars? What could you do with a bunch of old calendars?

6 Research the history of the calendar. Who invented it and for what purpose?

7 If you were going to create an original calendar, what theme or topic would you choose? Develop your idea into a report, a project, or a display with a calendar format.

8 What would life be like without calendars to help us keep track of time, dates, and events?

Word Power

1 Define and give examples of an oxymoron.

2 Give some examples of jargon used by students of your age. Then give words or phrases used by people of another generation to express the same ideas.

3 Make a list of words commonly overworked in speaking and writing. Supply an alternative for each word.

4 Define and give examples of synonyms, antonyms, and homonyms.

5 Name as many words as you can that could be used to express happiness or joy.

6 Name as many words as you can that could be used to express gloom and despair.

7 List at least twenty words or phrases that you need to be able to use to be a successful math student. Look up the meaning of any that you do not know.

8 List adjectives and adverbs that you use in daily conversation. Beside each word, write a more active or alive word that would make you a more interesting conversationalist.

9 Name as many prefixes as possible. Tell what each one means and supply a word that uses each.

10 Name as many suffixes as possible. Tell what each one means and supply a word that uses each.

11 Make an alphabetical listing of as many descriptive words as possible.

12 List twenty or more word categories that you normally use in class assignments. Try to name at least six words for each category.

13 Write down as many rhyming words as you can in two minutes. Create a poem, using only the words on your list plus three additional ones.

14 Make a list of at least twenty-five careers of interest to you. Write one or more unusual synonyms for each career.

15 Look in today's newspaper for words frequently used in ads. Find the most overused words and give reasons for their use.

16 Write a thank-you letter to someone in your school who deserves appreciation. Use at least ten words you've never used in a letter.

17 Select a "feeling word" and write it decoratively, "as it feels." Use this "feeling illustration" as the basis of a collage.

18 List ten or more words from your science textbook that have meanings you do not know. Find the meanings in a dictionary or thesaurus.

19 Develop a picture dictionary for a younger child using animal words, environmental words, weather and climate words, or plant words.

20 Define and give examples of metaphors and similes.

Speak Up

1 List suggestions for effective public speaking. Use your list to create a poster entitled "Speaker's Tip Sheet."	**2** Compare and contrast rules for a debate and rules for a persuasive lecture.	**3** Create a five-minute warmup activity to use for audience involvement before a lecture.	**4** Develop an agenda for a club meeting. Remember the call to order, officer's reports, old and new business, and adjournment.	**5** Review **Robert's Rules of Order** before developing a set of rules for conducting an orderly class meeting.
6 Present a lively skit showing what could happen when a meeting is held with no rules of order.	**7** Make a list of persuasive words that might be used by a speaker to convince an audience to accept a point of view.	**8** Present a lecturette to demonstrate the use of a math concept or procedure to your class.	**9** Agree or disagree with this statement: **"Poor listeners make poor speakers."** Justify your position.	**10** Extemporaneous speaking is considered by many people to be the most demanding of all forms of public speaking. Explore this belief and judge your own ability to speak extemporaneously.
11 Develop a detailed outline of a thirty-minute speech promoting conservation of your community's natural resources.	**12** Create a set of stretch-and-bend exercises to relieve tension in the middle of a long speech. Include verbal instructions for the exercises.	**13** Create a set of visual props to accompany a lecture on a topic of social concern to people of your age.	**14** Decide which would better portray the need for good sportsmanship to your classmates: a skit, lecture, rap, or slide show. Explain your choice.	**15** Tell why a sense of humor is important to public speakers. Tell how speakers can insert humor into their presentations.
16 Rate the following aids according to how useful each would be in developing speaking presentations: dictionary, encyclopedias, thesaurus, speaker's guide, and library card catalog. Explain the use of each in justifying your rating scale.	**17** Would you rather listen to the radio or watch television to learn about world news? Explain your choice.	**18** Plan and outline a class presentation to demonstrate how to do something (an art project, game, cooking, etc.).	**19** Give clear, concise directions for getting to a specific destination from where you are now.	**20** Write a creative story entitled "The Worst Speech I Ever Heard in My Entire Lifetime and Why I Had to Sit through It."

Use Your Imagination . . . .

1 Tell what would happen if all the clocks in the world were stopped for seventy-two hours.	**2** Write ten questions (with answers) for a "things you never knew" game about your school.	**3** Name at least ten substitutes for shoes.	**4** Create a theme, name, menu, and advertising slogan for a new fast food restaurant.	**5** Plan a trip to another planet. Include time frame, supplies, and daily schedules in your plan.
6 Use one of these titles for a creative story: **The Enormous Emerald The Elegant Extravert The Elusive Envelope The Envious Elf**	**7** List as many continents, countries, and cities as you can that begin with any one letter of the alphabet (your choice).	**8** Create a brand-new educational toy for preschool children. Sketch it, describe it, and give rules for its use.	**9** Create a wordfind puzzle with words related to the preservation of endangered plant and animal species.	**10** Develop a collage using triangles, rectangles, squares, and circles.
11 Write an original song or poem to promote respect for cultural diversity.	**12** List as many uses as you can think of for ice cubes.	**13** Illustrate one of these idioms or one of your own: **"Take the first fork in the road"** or **"I have a frog in my throat."**	**14** Write a letter to the school superintendent in support of banishing formal testing in the school system. Suggest an alternative.	**15** Make up a new recipe for broccoli and supply ten good reasons for eating it.
16 Create a television situation comedy about the day when fish could fly, potatoes grew as big as pumpkins, and baby chicks could talk.	**17** Make up an original jumprope rhyme or jingle using multiplication facts.	**18** Design a house for a family of four living in the year 2999. Write the building specifications.	**19** Use what you have learned about the universe to write a space fantasy featuring you as the main character.	**20** Make signs, posters, bumper stickers, and an advertising billboard to tell your community how great your school is.

Personal Publishing Project

1 Do some research to find out about how a book is made. Learn about right and left pages, usual numbers of pages, and parts of a book such as title page, copyright page, etc.	**2** This day is for dreaming! What kind of book (or poem or story) would you like to publish? Jot down ideas in a notebook.	**3** Take a trip to the library and/or bookstore to look at books that are similar to the one you want to publish. Pay attention to format, design, illustration, binding, etc.	**4** Find out what **public domain** means. Decide if you want to publish a story, such as a fairy tale, that is in the public domain. If not, write your own story!	**5** Continue writing (or key in your public domain story). Let your thoughts and words flow. This is not the time to criticize your work!
6 Continue writing and/or entering text. Use a computer if you have access to one. If not, type or neatly handprint your text.	**7** Take a break from writing and begin to think about format and design. As you design your book, use what you know about the parts of a book: title page, copyright page, right and left facing pages, etc.	**8** Go back to your first piece of writing and look at it with a fresh eye. Polish it, then give to someone else to read.	**9** Talk about your writing with the person who read it, or go over the person's notes. Make decisions about which criticism is valid and which is not. Revise your writing accordingly.	**10** Begin to work on rough sketches for illustrations for your story. By this time you should know your book's size, how many pages it will have, and how illustrations will fit with the text.
11 Another method of acquiring illustrations is to work with another student, perhaps one with special art talent. If you choose this method, work together to achieve final art that fits well with the book's concept.	**12** Work on the final art for your illustrations.	**13** Continue to work on final art. Continue to show your work to others.	**14** Pay special attention to cover design. Use eyecatching artwork and good design principles.	**15** Write several "blurbs" to go on the back of the book. If your book will have a jacket, write something about the book (and its author) for the flyleaf.
16 Gather together materials to create your book (paper, board, glue, etc.).	**17** Before assembling your book, look at the text one more time. Check it for good grammar and spelling. Show it to someone else who can proof your work.	**18** Assemble your book. You may choose to use a process as simple as stapling pages together, or a more elaborate bookbinding process that imitates professionally bound books.	**19** Ask someone to write a review of your book.	**20** How will you distribute your book? Will it be put on display? Put in the library? Even if it is primarily a classroom assignment, make sure you show it to others to enjoy.

Using Integrated Instructional Strategies to Promote Cooperative Learning and Group Interaction

OVERVIEW
Cooperative Learning Overview 74

THINK/PAIR/SHARE
Language Arts Activities 80

THREE-STEP INTERVIEW
Folklore 86

CIRCLE OF KNOWLEDGE
Language Arts Activities 91

TEAM LEARNING
Fun with Words 97

CO-OP CO-OP
Gods and Goddesses 102

NUMBERED HEADS TOGETHER
Paragraph Power 104

ROUND TABLE
Literary Analysis 106

JIGSAW
Poetry Portraits 116

Using Cooperative Learning
as an Instructional Tool

A cooperative learning group is an excellent means of teaching basic skills or reinforcing important concepts in any content area. Cooperative learning, as described by Johnson and Johnson (1991), involves teamwork within small groups of heterogeneous students working in a structured setting, with assigned roles, and towards a common goal. The five elements that distinguish cooperative learning from traditional group work, according to the Johnsons, are:

POSITIVE INTERDEPENDENCE
. . . requires the students to assist one another in the learning process through common goals, joint rewards, shared resources, and specified role assignments.

FACE-TO-FACE INTERACTION
. . . requires the students to actively engage in discussion, problem solving, decision making, and mutual assignment completion.

INDIVIDUAL ACCOUNTABILITY
. . . requires the student to carry through on "his or her share of the work" and to contribute as an individual to the established common goals.

INTERPERSONAL SKILLS
. . . require group members to learn and apply a range of communication and active learning skills.

GROUP PROCESSING
. . . requires the students to consistently evaluate their ability to function as a group by obtaining legitimate feedback and reinforcement.

Although roles for cooperative learning groups vary, the most common roles are those of Recorder, Time Keeper, Manager, Gopher, and Encourager.

Rules for cooperative learning groups vary too, but the most common are the following:

1   **Students assume responsibility for their own behavior.**

2   **Students are accountable for contributing to the group's work.**

3   **Students are expected to help any group member who needs it.**

4   **Students ask the teacher for help only as a last resort.**

5   **Students may not "put down" or embarrass any group member.**

The size of cooperative groups can range from pairs and trios to larger groups of four to six. It is important to keep in mind, however, that the smaller the group, the more chance there is for active participation and interaction of all group members. Groups of two, for example, can theoretically "have the floor" for fifty percent of the learning time, while groups of five can theoretically do so for only twenty percent of the learning time, if all are to contribute to the group goal in an equitable fashion. Likewise, it is important to note that groups should most often be put together in a random or arbitrary fashion so that the combination of group members varies with each task and so that group members represent a more heterogeneous type of placement. This can be done in a variety of ways ranging from "drawing names out of a hat" to having kids "count off" so those with the same numbers can be grouped together.

There are many different formats that can be used with cooperative learning groups and each of them has its advantages.

On the following pages are descriptions to provide teachers with several structures that can be used in developing lesson plans around the cooperative learning method of instruction. Several applications for each of these structures can be found on pages 80 through 118.

THINK/PAIR/SHARE

In this format, the teacher gives the students a piece of information through a delivery system such as the lecturette, videotape, or transparency talk. The teacher then poses a higher-order question related to the information presented. Students are asked to reflect on the question and write down their responses after appropriate waiting time has passed. Students are then asked to turn to a partner and share responses. Teachers should prepare a plan ahead of time for ways in which students will be paired. If time allows, one pair of students may share ideas with another pair of students, making groups of four. Sufficient time for discussion and for all students to speak should be allowed. The advantages of this structure are:

- It is easy to use in large classes.

- It gives students time to reflect on course content.

- It allows students time to rehearse and embellish information before sharing with a small group or entire class.

- It fosters long-term retention of course content.

THREE-STEP INTERVIEW

In this format, the teacher presents students with information on a given topic or concept. The teacher then pairs students and asks a question about the information such as: "What do you think about . . . ?" or "How would you describe . . . ?" or "Why is this important . . . ?" Each member of the pair responds to the question while the other practices active listening skills, knowing that he or she will have to speak for his or her partner at a later time. Each pair is then grouped with another pair so that each group member becomes one of four members. Person Two answers the question using the words of Person One and Person Three answers the questions using the words of Person Four. Roles are exchanged, and this process is repeated four times. The advantages of this structure are:

- It fosters important listening skills.

- It forces the student to articulate a position or response from another person's perspective.

- It presents multiple interpretations of the same information.

CIRCLE OF KNOWLEDGE

The teacher places students in groups of four to six. A Recorder (who does not participate in the brainstorming because he or she is busy writing down responses) is assigned to each group by the teacher. A question or prompt is given. Everyone takes a turn to brainstorm and respond to the question or prompt, beginning with the person to the left of the Recorder. Responses should be given by individuals around the circle, in sequence, as many times as possible within a five-minute period of time or "until the well runs dry." Group Recorders are asked to report responses from their group to the whole class without repeating an idea already shared by another group Recorder. These collective responses are written on the chalkboard or on a piece of chart paper for all to see.

- This structure is good for review and reinforcement of learned material or for introducing a new unit of study.

- It gives every student an equal opportunity to respond and participate.

- It lets a student know in advance when it is his or her turn to contribute.

- It does not judge the quality of a student's response.

- It fosters listening skills through the rule of "no repetition of the same or similar ideas in either the brainstorming or sharing processes."

TEAM LEARNING

In this cooperative learning format, the teacher places students in groups of four. Each group is given a Recording Sheet and asked to appoint a Recorder and to assign other group roles. The Recording Sheet is a "group worksheet" that contains four to six questions or tasks to be completed. A team must reach consensus on a group response for each question/task only after each member has provided input. The Recorder writes down the consensus response. When the work is finished, all team members review the group responses and sign the Recording Sheet to show they have read it, edited it, and agreed with it. These papers are collected and graded. The advantages of this structure are:

- Students build, criticize (positively), and edit one another's ideas.

- Teachers only have a few papers to grade since there is only one per group rather than one per student.

- Students collaborate on the work for a group grade rather than compete for an individual grade.

A wide variety of springboards can be used for Team Learning questions/tasks such as math manipulatives (tangrams, meter sticks, protractors), reading materials (poems, editorials, short stories), science tools (charts/graphs, rock collections, lab manuals), or social studies aids (globes, maps, compasses).

CO-OP CO-OP

The teacher places students in cooperative learning groups, each with four to six members. Group membership can be determined by grouping students who share specific areas of interest in the unit of study.

The teacher first delivers a classroom presentation or leads a large group discussion designed to introduce the topic. This introductory activity will provide all students with a common understanding of the basic objectives for the unit. Next, the teacher provides a list of possible topics and subtopics appropriate for the unit of study. Once the cooperative learning groups are formed, each group selects one of the major topics for in-depth study. Make sure that no two groups have the same topic. Each individual student within a group selects an appropriate subtopic and prepares a short report on that subtopic to present to other group members. Each group, or team, then prepares a group presentation for the class. Team presentations are followed by evaluation. (1) Team presentations are evaluated by the class; (2) Individual contributions are evaluated by the members of each team. (3) Each individual's written contribution is evaluated by the teacher. The advantages of this structure are:

- It is suitable for groups working on collaborative projects, papers, or reports.
- It offers three types of evaluation, covering individual, small group, and large group contributions.
- Group members share common interests as the basis for work.

NUMBERED HEADS TOGETHER

The teacher forms groups of four members each. Each student is assigned a number within the group: 1, 2, 3, or 4. The teacher asks a question, gives a command, or presents a problem to solve, and then calls out a number for student response. If the called-out number is, say, number 3, the number 3 students from each group raise hands to be called on, to go to the board to write an answer, to state an answer orally, or to record an answer on individual slates. Points are awarded to groups for correct answers by individual team members. The advantages of this structure are:

- It is useful for reviewing learned material or for checking for student understanding of material.
- It promotes positive interdependence because it is everyone's responsibility to be prepared for every question/command/problem since no one knows which number will be called by the teacher.
- It fosters cooperative competition—every group can be a winner.
- It requires application of higher-order thinking skills.
- It is useful for reviewing material or practicing a skill.
- It fosters interdependence among group members.

ROUND TABLE

In this cooperative learning format, the teacher forms groups of four to six members. The teacher gives each group of students a comprehensive problem to solve, an open-ended question to answer, or a complex activity to complete. Each student is asked to consider the assigned tasks and to record an individual response in writing. The key factor is that a group is given only one sheet of paper and one pencil. The sheet of paper is moved to the left around the group and, one at a time, each group member records his or her response on the sheet. No one is allowed to skip a turn. The students then determine an answer to represent the group's thinking, constructing a response that synthesizes many ideas. An optional final stage: each group shares its collective response with the whole class. The advantages of this structure are:

- It requires application of higher-order thinking skills.

- It is useful for reviewing material or practicing a skill.

- It fosters interdependence among group members.

JIGSAW

In this structure, the teacher forms home cooperative learning groups of six members and assigns each member a number from 1 to 6. Each member of a home group leaves that group to join another made up of one member of each of the other groups. The purpose of this arrangement is to have groups of students become experts on one aspect of a problem to be solved or a piece of information to be analyzed. In essence, Jigsaw is so named because it is a strategy in which each member of a given group gets only one piece of the information or problem-solving puzzle at a time. The teacher presents each of the "expert groups" with a portion of a problem or one piece of an information paper to research, study, and acquire in-depth knowledge. Each "expert" member is responsible for mastering the content or concepts and developing a strategy for teaching it to the home team. The "expert" then returns to the home team and teaches all other members about his or her information or problem, and learns the information presented by the other group members as well. The advantages of this structure are:

- It fosters individual accountability through use of the "expert" role.

- It promotes group interdependence through "teaching and learning" processes.

- It encourages the use of high-quality communication skills through the teacher and learner roles.

Student Directions:

THINK/PAIR/SHARE

A **Think/Pair/Share** activity is designed to provide you and a partner with some "food for thought" on a given topic so that you can both write down your ideas and share your responses with each other. Follow these directions when completing the Recording Sheet.

1 Listen carefully to the information on the topic of the day presented by your teacher. Take notes on the important points.

2 Use the Recording Sheet to write down the assigned question or task as well as your response to that question or task.

3 Discuss your ideas with a partner and record something of interest he or she shared.

4 If time permits, you and your partner should share your combined ideas with another pair of students.

5 Determine why "two, three, or four heads are better than one."

A List of Possible
Think/Pair/Share
Springboards for Language Arts

GRAMMAR

1. Tell some major rules for use of the comma.

2. Show when it is appropriate to use a colon in a sentence and when to use a semicolon by giving examples.

3. Discuss the times when nouns are always capitalized.

4. Determine why good grammar in speaking and writing is important.

5. How should quotations in a sentence be punctuated?

6. Which punctuation mark has the most personality—the period, the question mark, or the exclamation mark? Why?

7. Define **acronym**. Give examples of acronyms.

8. When is it appropriate to abbreviate words and when is it not?

9. Discuss the mistakes in grammar which you and others most commonly make in your writing.

10. Name the eight parts of speech and give an example of each one.

11. Try using each of the following sets of troublesome words in a sentence correctly: **sit/set, lie/lay, there/their/they're, here/hear, its/it's, good/well,** and **two/too/to.**

12. What does **agreement** mean when you are discussing tenses? When you are discussing singular and plural nouns and verbs? What are some ways that you can make sure nouns, pronouns, and verbs agree with one another when writing sentences?

POETRY

1. Identify your favorite poem and tell why you like it.

2. Are nursery rhymes a form of poetry? Why or why not?

3. Discuss how figurative language is important when writing poetry.

4. Give an example of **alliteration.**

5. Make up several similes about yourself. (I am as funny as a . . . I am as serious as a . . .)

6. Explain **personification.** Think of some objects that would be fun to personify in a poem or story.

7. Think of some rhyming words for each of the following words and use them to create original couplets: **time, fall, run, know, night.**

8. Suppose you were a mountain. What things would make you happy and what things would make you sad?

9. Think of a metaphor to complete this statement: **"Freedom is . . ."**

10. How would you explain **meter** to another student?

11. Brainstorm a list of as many words as you can that are kinds of **onomatopoeia.**

12. Discuss themes that are commonly found in poetry.

13. Discuss the rhythm of **metered** poetry, and tell how certain types of poetry are associated with certain metrical patterns.

14. Discuss how poetry has been used to communicate throughout the ages, and how it has been used in different ways during different eras.

LITERATURE

1. What is your favorite literary genre? Why?

2. Explain how literature is a part of culture.

3. Describe one of your favorite novels and its major characters.

4. Discuss why plot is so important in a good story. How does one determine the climax of the story?

5. Define the following terms and give an example of each: **point of view, mood, irony, foreshadowing,** and **flashback.**

6. Why is the setting important in a book?

7. Discuss whether a book must have conflict and resolution as part of its plot in order to be considered a good story.

8. What are some ways an author holds a reader's interest?

9. Discuss your favorite fairy tale character, tall tale character, and mythological character.

10. It has been said that storytelling is both an "art" and a "science." Tell whether you agree with this or not.

11. What book do you think should have been given the Newbery Award but was not? Give reasons for your answer.

12. What is the meaning of this statement? **"Without the love of books, the richest man is poor."**

13. Do you think a book should ever be banned for any reason?

14. What are the differences between "fine literature" and "popular fiction"? Is one type of literature more valuable than the other?

LIBRARY

1. Discuss the different types of information one can find in an atlas, an almanac, and an anthology.

2. Summarize how a thesaurus and a dictionary are alike and how they are different.

3. Describe how the resources of a modern library have changed over the years.

4. Discuss ways an encyclopedia can be used by students for research. Are there ways it can be misused?

5. Explain the purpose of a vertical file in the library media center.

6. When would you use the following references to help you with classroom assignments? *Reader's Guide to Periodical Literature, Guiness Book of World Records,* and *Webster's Geographical Dictionary.*

7. What type of fiction do you prefer? Why?

8. Discuss the types of library assignments that you most enjoy.

9. If you could read or write a biography of another person, who would you choose? Explain.

10. Discuss how children's picture books can be enjoyed by older students and adults as well as by young children.

11. It has been said that libraries and the printed word will become obsolete with the advance of technology. How do you feel about this prediction?

12. What would make a library more appealing to kids your age?

13. Do library skills that are necessary today differ from those that were necessary a generation ago? Give reasons for your answer.

Recording Sheet

Language Arts

NAME_____

DATE_____

QUESTION OR TASK TO BE COMPLETED: _____

_____
_____
_____
_____
_____
_____
_____
_____
_____

MY IDEAS ON THE TOPIC: _____

_____
_____
_____
_____
_____
_____
_____
_____
_____
_____
_____

IDEAS SHARED BY MY PARTNER(S): _____

_____
_____
_____
_____
_____
_____
_____
_____
_____
_____
_____
_____
_____

Student Directions:

THREE-STEP INTERVIEW

In the **Three-step Interview** activity, you will be given some information on a topic by your teacher, then you will work with a partner to discuss your ideas on the topic. You and your partner must take turns as active listener and as active speaker. Follow these directions in order to complete the Recording Sheets.

1 Work with an assigned partner and decide who will be the first speaker and who will be the first listener.

2 Read the Background Information on Folklore given to you by your teacher. Think carefully about the information.

3 Use the Recording Sheets to prepare your written responses to the six questions. You will use these responses as a basis for discussing the subject with your partner.

4 After talking to your partner while he or she carefully listens to your ideas, exchange roles and let your partner give responses while you listen intently. You may want to take some notes about what he or she tells you.

5 As time permits, you and your partner are to join another pair of students and share opinions and information about the world of folklore.

Background Information
Folklore

Folktales are stories of make-believe or fantasy that are handed down from generation to generation. They are important because they reflect cultural values and because they allow anecdotes and traditions to be passed on from grandparent to parent to child. Of no less importance is the folktale's function as entertaining story. Two fine examples of enchanting folktales are Hans Christian Andersen's "Thumbelina," whose theme is the common one of enchantment of tiny people, and the story of the long sleep in "Sleeping Beauty" by Perrault.

The transformation of animal into person, or person into animal, is an element common to many folktales. "Beauty and the Beast" and "The Frog Prince," both by the Grimm brothers, are well-known examples. Magic objects are important in many tales. The Japanese tale "The Dancing Kettle" is of a magic kettle that makes a fortune for a junkman.

A task or trial forms the plot of many a folktale, as a character tries to win a maiden, gain freedom from a sorcerer's spell, or achieve higher status. Sometimes a task is a penalty for bragging or misbehavior, as is the case in the old favorite "Rumpelstiltskin."

The antics of a simpleton in a folktale may provide humor, but the humor is rarely cruel or barbaric. Frequently a fool will win a prize or will be rewarded for stupidity. An American folktale called "Rusty Jack" is about a farmer's son who is wise enough to trick a woodsman into believing a crow talks. Through a series of events, Jack wins a beautiful girl in the end.

Many folktales tell of wishes granted to individuals who then waste the wishes by using them in anger or without thought. "The Three Wishes" is about a woodsman who wishes for a pudding. Another wish results in the pudding attaching itself to the end of his nose, while the third and final wish must be used to remove the pudding.

Some folktales are semi-realistic stories that have been embellished with exaggeration. Magic plays no part in these stories. "Dick Whittington and His Cat," a classic rags-to-riches story, is one of these folktales.

Recording Sheet, Page 1

NAME_____

Folklore

DATE_____

Use the information on folklore to answer these questions and to share thoughts with your partner. Be sure to record some of your partner's ideas as well as your own.

1. Outline a plot for a folktale that tells how a "tiny teenager" became a hero after he or she saved a life-sized friend from disaster.

YOUR THOUGHTS: _____

_____

_____

_____

_____

YOUR PARTNER'S THOUGHTS: _____

_____

_____

_____

_____

_____

2. Outline a plot for a folktale in which an animal is transformed into a teacher of English. What kind of animal will you select? What attributes does he or she have as a teacher?

YOUR THOUGHTS: _____

_____

_____

_____

_____

YOUR PARTNER'S THOUGHTS: _____

_____

_____

_____

_____

_____

Recording Sheet, Page 2
Folklore

3. Outline a plot for a folktale in which a task must be performed or a trial must be endured before a kid can accept the town's biggest award in sports or academics.

YOUR THOUGHTS: _____

_____

_____

_____

_____

_____

_____

YOUR PARTNER'S THOUGHTS: _____

_____

_____

_____

_____

_____

_____

4. Outline a plot for a folktale in which the "class clown" saves the day for all teachers, students, or parents.

YOUR THOUGHTS: _____

_____

_____

_____

_____

_____

_____

YOUR PARTNER'S THOUGHTS: _____

_____

_____

_____

_____

_____

Recording Sheet, Page 3
Folklore

5. Outline a plot for a folktale in which a young hero is granted three wishes to make him or her a better student, friend, or athlete, but everything goes wrong.

YOUR THOUGHTS: _____

_____
_____
_____
_____
_____
_____

YOUR PARTNER'S THOUGHTS: _____

_____
_____
_____
_____
_____
_____

6. Outline a plot for a folktale in which a school's entire student population received straight A's one semester.

YOUR THOUGHTS: _____

_____
_____
_____
_____
_____
_____

YOUR PARTNER'S THOUGHTS: _____

_____
_____
_____
_____
_____
_____

Student Directions:
CIRCLE OF KNOWLEDGE

A **Circle of Knowledge** activity provides a small group situation for brainstorming responses to a given question or prompt presented by the teacher. Follow these directions when completing the Recording Sheet.

1 Agree on a Recorder for your group. Direct the Recorder to write down the names of all group members and the assigned question or prompt in the appropriate sections of the Recording Sheet.

2 Share your responses to the question or prompt when it is your turn in the circle. Make sure you are ready to respond and that your ideas are recorded as given by the Recorder.

3 Assist the Recorder during the large-group sharing of all responses by helping him or her note which ideas have already been given by the other groups in the class and therefore should not be repeated when it is your group's turn to share.

4 Review the responses generated by both your group and the large group that have been recorded on the chalkboard, transparency, or chart paper.

5 Determine why "two, three, or four heads are better than one."

Recording Sheet

DATE_____

Circle of Knowledge

GROUP MEMBERS:

1. _____
2. _____
3. _____
4. _____
5. _____
6. _____

QUESTION OR PROMPT FOR BRAINSTORMING:

COLLECTIVE RESPONSES:

Sample Questions or Prompts for Circle of Knowledge Activities

LITERATURE

1. Name some favorite authors of novels you have read.

2. Name favorite characters from books you have read.

3. List characteristics of a good short story.

4. Write down the title of a book you might want to write in the future.

5. Name favorite nursery rhymes or fairy tales that were read to you as a child.

6. Identify famous characters from Greek or Roman mythology.

7. Identify famous characters from tall tales or legends.

8. What are the characteristics of a fable?

9. Select a novel. List the events of the plot in chronological order.

10. Identify settings from short stories or novels you have read.

11. Make up analogies.

12. Recite as many proverbs as you can.

13. Think of as many idioms as you can.

14. Write down as many images as you can create for each of the following starter statements:

    Friendship is like . . .
    School is like . . .
    Electricity is like . . .
    War is like . . .

15. Make up possible questions for the following answers. **Satire. Fiction. Nonfiction. Genre. Plot. Point of view.**

POETRY

1. Name a figure of speech and give an example of one.

2. Complete these similes:

   as stupid as . . .

   as scary as . . .

   as funny as . . .

   as simple as . . .

   as ridiculous as . . .

3. List your favorite poems from our study of poetry.

4. Think of words that rhyme with: **bright, cry, deep, ill, stone.**

5. Identify a poetry form and describe its pattern.

6. Write down **onomatopoeia** sounds.

7. Make up a short **alliterative** sentence.

8. List reasons people may or may not enjoy poetry.

9. Think of funny rhyming pairs such as "bear scare," "damp camp," or "loud crowd."

10. Give all of the possible questions for this answer: **Poetry.**

11. Name titles of poems that you have read or about which you know.

12. List things that "make a poem a poem."

13. Name common themes or topics of poems.

14. Make up second lines for a couplet that begins with:

    "If you want to have fun on a sunny day . . ."

    OR

    "I see the birds so high in the sky . . ."

15. Complete this starter statement: **"Beauty is . . ."**

GRAMMAR

1. List nouns (or verbs or adjectives) that you associate with each of the following: **circus, football game, school, museum, Thanksgiving, mountains.**

2. Think of four-syllable words.

3. List rules of punctuation.

4. Write down rules of capitalization.

5. Recite a tongue twister.

6. State facts about life in the United States.

7. Give opinions about life in the United States.

8. Use free-association thinking to come up with words associated with **happy** or **angry** or **sad.**

9. Think of words spelled with double consonants such as **pudding, apple, cheddar,** and **casserole.**

10. Name words with identical spellings that have different meanings such as "wind," "present," and "lead."

11. Write down some "Tom Swifties."

12. Think of synonyms for these tired words: **said, run,** and **walked.**

13. List a word with its **antonym** and/or its **synonym.**

14. Think of as many long words as you can that are often used in a short form such as **memo, flue, sitcom,** or **deli.**

READING, WRITING, AND LISTENING

1. Think of the advantages of being a good listener.

2. List barriers to good listening.

3. Name the characteristics of a good listener.

4. Give examples of words with prefixes and/or suffixes.

5. Make a list of contractions.

6. Write down short vowel words and/or long vowel words.

7. List words with initial consonant blends or final consonant blends.

8. List some good topics about which to write.

9. Write down as many types of writing as you can.

10. Think of items for a writing skills checklist or an editing skills checklist.

11. List spelling helps or hints to remember for good writing.

12. Name good descriptive words to use in your writing.

13. Write down "story starter" lines.

14. Think of as many ways as you can to make a book report.

15. Think of as many ways as you can to organize information (examples: an outline, a diagram).

Student Directions:
TEAM LEARNING

During a **Team Learning** activity, your cooperative learning group will respond collectively to questions and tasks. Assign the role of Recorder to one member of your group. The Recorder should follow these directions to complete the Recording Sheet:

1 Assign one of the following jobs to each member of your group so that each person has at least one job: Timekeeper, Coordinator, Checker, and Evaluator (some members may have more than one task to perform).

2 Distribute a copy of the Task Sheet to each group member and a copy of the Recording Sheet plus extra pieces of paper to the Recorder. Ask all to read the questions and tasks.

3 Discuss your ideas for each item and reach consensus on a group response for each item. The Recorder is to write down these collaborative responses to questions and tasks, supplementing the Recording Sheet with additional pieces of paper. The Coordinator is to facilitate the discussion. The Timekeeper is to keep track of the time allotted for the assignment. The Checker is to read through the responses orally, checking for grammar, comprehension, and consensus errors.

4 All cooperative learning group members are to sign their names at the bottom of the Recording Sheet, indicating agreement with the responses and acknowledging fair contributions to the work.

Recording Sheet, Page 1

DATE_____

Fun with Words

TEAM MEMBERS:

1. _____
2. _____
3. _____
4. _____
5. _____
6. _____

1 A compound word is one word made of two words that have been put together. Think of at least 10 compound words and write them down. Then add the first half of one compound word to the second half of another compound word. Write the new word and draw a symbol or picture of it to show its meaning.

   Examples: junkyard and farmhouse = junkhouse
   earthquake and boathouse = boatquake

_____

_____

_____

_____

_____

2 Homonyms are two words with two different spellings that are pronounced the same. Think of at least 10 pairs of homonyms and write them down. Then write several humorous sentences, intentionally using the wrong homonyms in each.

   Examples: We went to the see for a weak.
   No won herd the plain fly write buy.

_____

_____

_____

_____

_____

Fun with Words

3 Antonyms are words that mean the opposite of each other. A pair of antonyms can make an interesting title of a book. Think of at least 10 pairs of antonyms that would make good book titles. Write a one-sentence summary of the book's plot after each title.

Example: **Chief Follower**

This is the story of a special leader who ruled his people by empowering them to make decisions which he then supported.

Recording Sheet, Page 3

Fun with Words

4 Synonyms are words that have similar meanings. Think of five different synonyms for each of the following words: **said, walked,** and **happy.** Then write sentences in which you might ordinarily use **said, walked,** or **happy,** but substitute some of your synonyms for these words.

Example: Sue scampered down the street, looking for her friend. She was ecstatic when she found Ellen at the corner drugstore. She whispered, "Let's stroll over to the mall. I have some spending money."

Recording Sheet, Page 4
Fun with Words

5 Idioms are expressions or sayings that are not meant to be taken literally. The words say one thing but mean another. Think of 10 different idioms and write them down. Then write what is meant by each idiom.

Example: Idiom—"My mother has a green thumb."
Meaning—"My mother is very good at working with plants in the garden. The plants in her garden are always green, healthy, and beautiful."

Student Directions:

CO-OP CO-OP ACTIVITY

During the **Co-Op Co-op** activity, you will work on a small group report that covers a major topic. Each member of your group will do some research and write about a subtopic of that major idea. Follow these directions when completing the Recording Sheet.

1 Listen to your teacher's introductory lecture on gods and goddesses of Mount Olympus.

2 The teacher will present your group with the following options for selecting a major topic (with corresponding subtopics) for study. Choose one of the major topics for your group, making sure that other groups in the class have not already taken your choice.

Major Topics:

Zeus and Hera
Poseidon and Hestia
Ares and Hades
Apollo and Athena
Hermes and Aphrodite
Hephaestus and Artemis

3 Once your major topic has been selected, divide subtopics among members of your small group so that each individual has a different one to research.

4 Conduct research on your subtopic and write your findings in a short report. The other group members should do the same with their subtopics.

5 When all reports are completed, present your ideas to one another in the small group.

6 Finally, combine the information from all of the reports in your small group to create a large group report. Working as a team, present this combined report to the entire class.

Recording Sheet   NAME_____

Gods and Goddesses
of Mount Olympus   DATE_____

Put a checkmark (√) next to the major topic your group has decided to report on. Put an "X" next to the subtopic you have chosen to research and about which you will write.

_____ ZEUS AND HERA

_____ Do some research to find out the definition and purpose of a myth and why a myth is interesting to read.

_____ Find out who Zeus and Hera were.

_____ Discover what Zeus and Hera did and for what they are best known.

_____ Get information that will help you describe Zeus and Hera.

_____ Find the symbols that are associated with Zeus and Hera. Find out why.

_____ Identify the Roman names of Zeus and Hera as well as the names of their parents.

_____ Discover some unusual facts about Zeus and Hera.

_____ POSEIDON AND HESTIA

_____ Do some research to get some information about the Olympians.

_____ Find out who Poseidon and Hestia were.

_____ Discover what Poseidon and Hestia did and for what they are best known.

_____ Get information that will help you describe Poseidon and Hestia.

_____ Find the symbols that are associated with Poseidon and Hestia. Find out why.

_____ Identify the Roman names of Poseidon and Hestia as well as the names of their parents.

_____ Discover some unusual facts about Poseidon and Hestia.

_____ ARES AND HADES

_____ Do some research to discover where and over whom the Olympians ruled.

_____ Find out who Ares and Hades were.

_____ Discover what Ares and Hades did and for what they are best known.

_____ Get information that will help you describe Ares and Hades.

_____ Find the symbols that are associated with Ares and Hades. Find out why.

_____ Identify the Roman names of Ares and Hades as well as the names of their parents.

_____ Discover some unusual facts about Ares and Hades.

_____ Apollo and Athena

_____ Do some research to find information about the Titans and their relationship to the Olympians.

_____ Find out who Apollo and Athena were.

_____ Discover what Apollo and Athena did and for what they are best known.

_____ Get information that will help you describe Apollo and Athena.

_____ Find the symbols that are associated with Apollo and Athena. Find out why.

_____ Identify the Roman names of Apollo and Athena as well as the names of their parents.

_____ Discover unusual facts about Apollo and Athena.

_____ Hermes and Aphrodite

_____ Do some research to find out what happened when Greece was conquered by the armies of Rome in 146 B.C.

_____ Find out who Hermes and Aphrodite were.

_____ Discover what Hermes and Aphrodite did and for what they are best known.

_____ Get information that will help you describe Hermes and Aphrodite.

_____ Find the symbols that are associated with Hermes and Aphrodite. Find out why.

_____ Identify the Roman names of Hermes and Aphrodite as well as the names of their parents.

_____ Discover some unusual facts about Hermes and Aphrodite.

_____ Hephaestus and Artemis

_____ Do some research to find out something about Roman mythology.

_____ Find out who Hephaestus and Artemis were.

_____ Discover what Hephaestus and Artemis did and for what they are best known.

_____ Get information that will help you describe Hephaestus and Artemis.

_____ Find the symbols that are associated with Hephaestus and Artemis. Find out why.

_____ Identify the Roman names of Hephaestus and Artemis as well as the names of their parents.

_____ Discover some unusual facts about Hephaestus and Artemis.

Student Directions:
NUMBERED HEADS TOGETHER

During the **Numbered Heads Together** activity, you will work in a small group of four and, one student at a time, give a response to a prompt issued by the teacher. Follow these directions to complete the Recording Sheet.

1 Assign the numbers **1** through **4** to the members of your group.

2 Decide on how each of you will respond to the prompt given by the teacher. Will you, and members of the other small groups who have the same number, respond by writing the answer on the chalkboard or by recording the answer on an individual slate?

3 The teacher will be giving you prompts as on the television game Jeopardy. The topic of today's Numbered Heads activity is "Paragraph Power." The teacher will give you the answer in the form of a term and, as on Jeopardy, you must respond by coming up with an appropriate question. When the teacher gives the class an answer, he or she will also call out a number for a student response. If, for example, the teacher calls out the number **3**, all of the number **3** students from all groups raise their hands to be called on, and simultaneously write their responses on the chalkboard or slate.

4 Points will be awarded to groups for correct answers by individual team members.

Recording Sheet   NAME_____

Paragraph Power

DATE_____

Use this sheet to practice for the Numbered Heads activity "Paragraph Power." Try to see how many of these answers you can give questions for, Jeopardy style. Example: If you are given the **answer** "root word," you might come up with one of the following **questions**: (1) What do we call the word "reliable" in "reliability"?; or (2) What is the main part of a word from which that word gets its meaning?; or (3) If we remove the prefix "im" from the word "improve," what do we call the word that remains?

1. ANSWER: Compound sentence.   **What is the question?**

_____

_____

2. ANSWER: Prefix.   **What is the question?**

_____

_____

3. ANSWER: Suffix.   **What is the question?**

_____

_____

4. ANSWER: Topic sentence.   **What is the question?**

_____

_____

5. ANSWER: Sentence fragment.   **What is the question?**

_____

_____

6. ANSWER: Declarative sentence.   **What is the question?**

_____

_____

7. ANSWER: Interrogative sentence.   **What is the question?**

_____

_____

8. ANSWER: Exclamatory sentence.   **What is the question?**

_____

_____

9. ANSWER: Paragraph.   **What is the question?**

_____

_____

Can you think of others?

©1996 by Incentive Publications, Inc., Nashville, TN.

Student Directions:
ROUND TABLE

During the **Round Table** activity, you and your assigned group will analyze a short story or a novel by recording individual responses to a set of questions "round robin" style. It is important that you read the same short story or novel so that you can build upon one another's ideas. Follow these directions when completing the Recording Sheets (there will be three sets of each recording sheet).

1 Decide on the order for recording responses. Who will go first, second, third, fourth, fifth, and sixth?

2 Use the Recording Sheets to write everybody's responses to all six questions. After the first person writes down his or her idea, the paper is moved to the left around the group. No one may skip a turn.

3 The paper should be passed around the group six times. Make sure that each member of the group responds to Question 1 only on the first round and Question 2 only on the second round, and so on.

4 One person in the group is responsible for completing information at the top of the Recording Sheet.

5 After all six questions have been answered by all six group members, the group should analyze the responses and synthesize the ideas into a comprehensive paragraph.

Recording Sheets

DATE_____

Literary Analysis

GROUP MEMBERS:

1. _____
2. _____
3. _____
4. _____
5. _____
6. _____

TITLE OF SHORT STORY/NOVEL: _____

AUTHOR OF SHORT STORY/NOVEL: _____

PUBLISHER AND COPYRIGHT
DATE OF SHORT STORY/NOVEL: _____

- -

STUDENT ONE RESPONSE

Question 1: What were the major strengths and weaknesses of the main characters (protagonist and antagonist) in this story?

- -

STUDENT TWO RESPONSE

Question 1: What were the major strengths and weaknesses of the main characters (protagonist and antagonist) in this story?

STUDENT THREE RESPONSE

Question 1: What were the major strengths and weaknesses of the main characters (protagonist and antagonist) in this story?

STUDENT FOUR RESPONSE

Question 1: What were the major strengths and weaknesses of the main characters (protagonist and antagonist) in this story?

STUDENT FIVE RESPONSE

Question 1: What were the major strengths and weaknesses of the main characters (protagonist and antagonist) in this story?

STUDENT SIX RESPONSE

Question 1: What were the major strengths and weaknesses of the main characters (protagonist and antagonist) in this story?

STUDENT ONE RESPONSE

Question 2: How would you describe the setting of this story?

STUDENT TWO RESPONSE

Question 2: How would you describe the setting of this story?

STUDENT THREE RESPONSE

Question 2: How would you describe the setting of this story?

STUDENT FOUR RESPONSE

Question 2: How would you describe the setting of this story?

STUDENT FIVE RESPONSE

Question 2: How would you describe the setting of this story?

STUDENT SIX RESPONSE

Question 2: How would you describe the setting of this story?

STUDENT ONE RESPONSE

Question 3: How would you describe the mood or atmosphere that was created by the characters, the setting, and the events of the story?

STUDENT TWO RESPONSE

Question 3: How would you describe the mood or atmosphere that was created by the characters, the setting, and the events of the story?

STUDENT THREE RESPONSE

Question 3: How would you describe the mood or atmosphere that was created by the characters, the setting, and the events of the story?

STUDENT FOUR RESPONSE

Question 3: How would you describe the mood or atmosphere that was created by the characters, the setting, and the events of the story?

STUDENT FIVE RESPONSE

Question 3: How would you describe the mood or atmosphere that was created by the characters, the setting, and the events of the story?

STUDENT SIX RESPONSE

Question 3: How would you describe the mood or atmosphere that was created by the characters, the setting, and the events of the story?

STUDENT ONE RESPONSE

Question 4: What was the major conflict in the story and how was it resolved?

STUDENT TWO RESPONSE

Question 4: What was the major conflict in the story and how was it resolved?

STUDENT THREE RESPONSE

Question 4: What was the major conflict in the story and how was it resolved?

STUDENT FOUR RESPONSE

Question 4: What was the major conflict in the story and how was it resolved?

STUDENT FIVE RESPONSE

Question 4: What was the major conflict in the story and how was it resolved?

STUDENT SIX RESPONSE

Question 4: What was the major conflict in the story and how was it resolved?

STUDENT ONE RESPONSE

Question 5: What was the point of view or angle of narration used to tell this story?

STUDENT TWO RESPONSE

Question 5: What was the point of view or angle of narration used to tell this story?

STUDENT THREE RESPONSE

Question 5: What was the point of view or angle of narration used to tell this story?

STUDENT FOUR RESPONSE

Question 5: What was the point of view or angle of narration used to tell this story?

STUDENT FIVE RESPONSE

Question 5: What was the point of view or angle of narration used to tell this story?

STUDENT SIX RESPONSE

Question 5: What was the point of view or angle of narration used to tell this story?

STUDENT ONE RESPONSE

Question 6: How would you rate this story on a scale of 1 to 5? Give one reason for your rating. 1 = poor 3 = okay 5 = excellent

STUDENT TWO RESPONSE

Question 6: How would you rate this story on a scale of 1 to 5? Give one reason for your rating. 1 = poor 3 = okay 5 = excellent

STUDENT THREE RESPONSE

Question 6: How would you rate this story on a scale of 1 to 5? Give one reason for your rating. 1 = poor 3 = okay 5 = excellent

STUDENT FOUR RESPONSE

Question 6: How would you rate this story on a scale of 1 to 5? Give one reason for your rating. 1 = poor 3 = okay 5 = excellent

STUDENT FIVE RESPONSE

Question 6: How would you rate this story on a scale of 1 to 5? Give one reason for your rating. 1 = poor 3 = okay 5 = excellent

STUDENT SIX RESPONSE

Question 6: How would you rate this story on a scale of 1 to 5? Give one reason for your rating. 1 = poor 3 = okay 5 = excellent

Student Directions:
JIGSAW ACTIVITY

During the **Jigsaw** activity you will work in a group of six in order to learn something new about poetry, and then teach this information to members of your home group. Follow these directions in order to complete the Recording Sheet.

1 Assign a number from one through six to each member of your home group.

2 With the help of your teacher, give each member of your group his or her appropriately numbered poetry portrait from the following pages. Don't let anyone see any poetry portrait except his or her own.

3 When the teacher gives you the signal, locate the other people in small home groups in your classroom who have a number the same as yours. Meet with them and together learn the information discussed in your poetry portrait so that each of you becomes an "expert" on its content. Once you have learned this information, have the group decide on a strategy for teaching it to the other members of your home group.

4 Return to your home team and teach all of the other members about your poetry portrait, and learn the information in their poetry portraits as well.

Recording Sheets

Poetry Portraits

DATE_____

HOME GROUP MEMBERS:

STUDENT **1** _____

STUDENT **2** _____

STUDENT **3** _____

STUDENT **4** _____

STUDENT **5** _____

STUDENT **6** _____

Cut the poetry portraits into six different sections. Give each section to the appropriate person in your group. Meet with the other students in the class who have a number the same as yours and learn the information presented in the poetry portrait.

STUDENT **1** **Writing a Cinquain**

A **cinquain** is a five-line stanza with a specified number of syllables in each line. It was invented by Adelaide Crapsey, who was influenced by the Japanese haiku. The pattern of syllables for the cinquain is:

   Line 1 (same as title) has one word of two syllables.
   Line 2 describes the title in two words that have four syllables between them.
   Line 3 has three words that express action and has a total of six syllables.
   Line 4 has four words that express feeling, with a total of eight syllables.
   Line 5 has one two-syllable word referring to the title.

Title: | |
| |

USE THIS PATTERN TO CREATE AN ORIGINAL CINQUAIN!

STUDENT **2** **Writing a Limerick**

A limerick is a traditional humorous form of poetry with five lines. Lines 1, 2, and 5 are the longer lines (6-10 syllables each), and they rhyme. Lines 3 and 4 rhyme with each other. They are shorter lines, having only 5-7 syllables each. Edward Lear (1812-1888) is credited with making the limerick a popular form of poetry.

USE THIS PATTERN TO CREATE AN ORIGINAL LIMERICK!

117

STUDENT **3** **Writing a Free Verse Poem**

Free verse poetry is written with no set form. It does not have a specific rhyme, pattern, or set of rules. This form of poetry gives the poet much freedom to experiment with thoughts, feelings, and ideas.

USE THIS POETIC FREEDOM TO CREATE A FREE VERSE POEM!

STUDENT **4** **Writing a Clerihew**

A clerihew is a special type of rhymed poetry that was created by an Englishman named Edmund Clerihew Bentley (1875-1956). A clerihew is always about a person (living or dead), has four lines, is usually humorous, and follows this pattern:

   Line 1 contains the name of the person in the poem.
   Lines 1 and 2 rhyme.
   Lines 3 and 4 rhyme.

USE THIS PATTERN TO CREATE AN ORIGINAL CLERIHEW!

STUDENT **5** **Writing a Tanka**

The tanka is a form of Japanese poetry similar to the haiku. The tanka was once used as a courtship ritual in Japan. The man would write the first three lines and give the poem to the lovely lady he wished to court. If the lady was interested, she would finish the poem by adding two lines and returning it to the man, who would write the final line. There are 5 syllables in each of lines 1 and 3, and 7 syllables in each of lines 2, 4, and 5.

USE THIS PATTERN TO CREATE AN ORIGINAL TANKA!

STUDENT **6** **Writing an Acrostic**

An acrostic was a favorite poetry form used centuries ago in the ancient cultures of Latin, Hebrew, and Greek. The form is usually unrhymed, and when the poem is complete, the first letters of the lines, when read vertically, should spell out a word, phrase, or sentence related to the poem's subject.

USE THIS PATTERN TO CREATE AN ORIGINAL ACROSTIC!

118

Using Integrated Instructional Strategies to Facilitate Authentic Assessment

OVERVIEW
Authentic Assessment 120
GUIDELINES AND SPRINGBOARDS
Journal Writing Guidelines 122
Springboards for Journal Writing 124
Springboards for Student Products 127
Springboards for Student Performances 129
SAMPLE PORTFOLIO
Interdisciplinary Unit in Language Arts 131
Portfolio Rubric/Conference Questions 140

An Overview of Authentic Assessment

In comparison with traditional types of assessment, assessment practices today emphasize more authentic ways to demonstrate that student learning has taken place. There is less assessment of the recall of information and more of the processing of information. Collecting evidence about a student over time in realistic settings is the best way to document growth and acquisition of both skills and content.

Product, performance, and portfolio assessment offer alternative assessment methods They are all more authentic than traditional methods because they:

- require collaboration among student, teacher, and peers;
- encourage student ownership through self-assessment;
- set flexible time limits;
- are scored through multifaceted systems;
- allow for student strengths and weaknesses;
- make use of individual learning styles and interests; and
- minimize competition.

In short, authentic assessment is designed to reflect real-world applications of knowledge whenever possible.

PRODUCT ASSESSMENT
. . . requires the student to produce a concrete end result. This can take many forms, ranging from a videotape or experiment to an exhibit or report.

PERFORMANCE ASSESSMENT
. . . requires the student to actively demonstrate a set of skills and processes while performing a predetermined task.

PORTFOLIO ASSESSMENT
. . . requires the student to maintain a collection of artifacts that reflects the student's overall efforts, progress, and achievements in one or more areas. It is important to note that both products and performances can and should become artifacts contained within the portfolio itself.

Assessment is also made more authentic through the consistent use of rubrics and metacognitive reflections throughout the assessment experience.

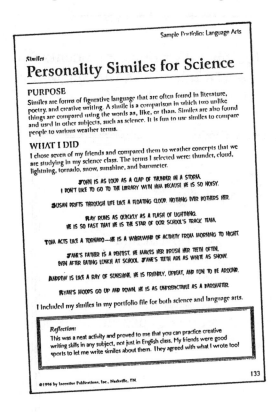

Rubrics are checklists that contain sets of criteria for measuring the elements of a product, performance, or portfolio. They can be designed as a qualitative measure (holistic rubric) to gauge overall performance to a prompt, or they can be designed as a quantitative measure (analytic rubric) to award points for each of several elements in a response to a prompt.

Metacognitive reflections are self-assessment observations and statements made by the individual student about each product or performance that he or she has completed. These reflections become part of the portfolio contents.

Although authentic assessment is designed to enhance and support the curriculum rather than dictate or limit the curriculum, it should be noted that more traditional means of measurement such as paper/pencil quizzes, standardized achievement exams, and objective end-of-chapter tests continue to play an important role in today's assessment practices. They should become one type of artifact included in the portfolio or one type of grade assigned to a performance or one type of measure used to determine the value of a product.

The following pages of this section provide the reader with a sample portfolio in language arts for a typical middle level student. This prototype is intended to show how authentic assessment—in the form of product, performance, and portfolio samples—can be used effectively to document student growth and achievement over time. It also contains student reflections and self-assessments that are intended to realistically appraise how the student is doing based on his or her own judgment in collaboration with the judgment of others, including the teacher.

Journal Writing Guidelines

Teachers may choose to use writing prompts for journal writing, or students may choose or suggest topics of their own. It is important, however, that all journal entries serve a purpose and that they be taken seriously.

PURPOSE

It is important to determine the purpose of a particular student journal assignment. Journals can and should be used for many different purposes. A journal can be:

a. a place for students to write down their personal responses to a textbook assignment, group discussion, independent research, or viewing of audiovisual resource.

b. a sourcebook or collection of ideas, thoughts, and opinions.

c. a place to write out first drafts of papers and assignments.

d. a place in which to record observations and questions about something read, written, or discussed.

e. a record-keeping tool that can help one keep track of what and how much was read on a topic, as well as personal perspectives on those readings.

f. a reference file to help teacher and student monitor individual growth and development.

g. a way for students to "dialogue" in written form with their teachers and peers.

Journals can be used every day or several times a week. They are generally kept in a separate notebook. In some cases, journals might be recorded on an audiotape (for students with special needs, for example).

Suggest to students that maintaining a journal is like keeping a photograph album because they are capturing pictures and/or slices of a given class or course. These snapshots will vary from "closeups" of a single topic to a "wide-angle lens view" of a broad topic.

The journal should be a place where students are encouraged to vary the style of their writing, ranging from nonstop, stream-of-consciousness writing to planned, organized essays.

Journal writing should be limited to approximately 10 minutes in length at any given time to achieve maximum effectiveness. Five minutes doesn't give the student enough time to get high-quality ideas on paper, and 15 minutes is too long a period to maintain a flow of high-quality ideas.

Journal entries should receive feedback in some formal or informal way. Feedback methods might include:

a. sharing journal entries with a peer or small group of peers in a Think/Pair/Share activity.

b. reading journal entries aloud to the class on a voluntary basis.

c. turning journal entries in to the teacher for written comments.

d. discussing journal entries with the teacher in a conference setting.

e. taking journal entries home for parent reading and input.

f. analyzing and answering one's own journal entry one or more days after the entry was recorded. This will allow for acknowledgment of personal changes in perspective and reflections based on new observations or information.

Some general types of journal writing tasks might be:

a. reactions to points or ideas that the student strongly supports or with which the student strongly disagrees.

b. questions about concepts that the student finds confusing.

c. paraphrases of complex ideas that the student finds interesting.

d. student comments that reflect personal experiences.

e. discussions that focus on the significance of the material read.

f. reflections on information that challenges a student's beliefs or value system.

Springboards for Journal Writing

REFLECTION STARTER STATEMENTS

1. Something important I learned from today's lesson is . . .
2. A question I have from today's discussion is . . .
3. Multiple meanings for the words/ideas/concepts we learned today are . . .
4. The answer is . . . Questions I can think of in response to this answer are . . .
5. Some different ways to view a . . . might be . . .
6. I wonder if . . .
7. When I think about the videotape (book, movie), I am surprised that . . .
8. A . . . is like a . . . because . . .
9. Some new terms I need to remember are . . .
10. The steps I followed in solving my problem (or completing my assignment) were . . .

SPRINGBOARDS FOR CRITICAL THINKING

1. **HOW ABOUT . . .**

   How about writing a friendly letter to someone you know?

   How about creating a sentence with an increasing number of syllables for each word?

2. **WHAT IF . . .**

   What if books could only be obtained electronically?

   What if you owned a pencil that would never write a mistake?

3. **CAN YOU . . .**

   Can you think of five good questions to ask a poet laureate?

   Can you rewrite the lyrics to a favorite nursery rhyme?

4. **WILL YOU . . .**

   Will you interview a peer and record your results in a written dialogue with correct punctuation?

   Will you invent a new type of spelling bee or grammar competition?

SPRINGBOARDS FOR CREATIVE THINKING

1. **YOU ARE AN ADVISOR.**

   What advice would you give to a young author?

   What advice would you give a novice public speaker?

2. **YOU ARE AN IMPROVER.**

   How would you improve book report assignments?

   How would you improve the teaching of English in the middle school?

3. **YOU ARE A DESIGNER.**

   Design a new poetry form or rhyming pattern.

   Design a lesson plan to teach students about parts of speech.

4. **YOU ARE A WORD SPECIALIST.**

   Write down all the words you associate with an airport.

   Write down all the overused words you can think of and substitute a more interesting word for each one.

5. **YOU ARE A PROBLEM SOLVER.**

   What would you do if you found yourself responsible for planning a grammar party for all the kids in your school?

   What would you do if you saw someone cheating on an English test?

6. **YOU ARE A WRITER.**

   Write a business letter to a publisher of teenage novels to tell how you feel about the publisher's authors.

   Write a list of words that conjure up bad or negative connotations such as the words "ugly" and "prejudice."

7. **YOU ARE AN IDEA PERSON.**

   Think of ten different messages for a box of fortune cookies.

   Think up poetry rhymes or couplets for each letter of the alphabet to be used in a children's ABC book.

8. **YOU ARE AN INFORMATION GIVER.**

   Write down five pieces of information that you have learned about the parts of a novel.

   Write what you know about the major elements of poetry.

SPRINGBOARDS BASED ON BLOOM'S TAXONOMY ≡

KNOWLEDGE LEVEL JOURNAL ENTRIES

a. Locate and define five to ten rules for forming plurals of words.

b. Record as many examples of idioms as you can find.

COMPREHENSION LEVEL JOURNAL ENTRIES

a. Summarize what you know about the construction of a good paragraph.

b. Give one example of a compound sentence and one example of a complex sentence.

APPLICATION LEVEL JOURNAL ENTRIES

a. Discuss situations in which the use of bad grammar is harmful.

b. Organize a panel discussion on the most common errors that students make in their writing and what can be done to avoid these mistakes.

ANALYSIS LEVEL JOURNAL ENTRIES

a. Debate the pros and cons of using word processors in the classroom to teach writing skills. Try to list at least three arguments for and three arguments against this practice in preparing for the debate.

b. Survey members of your class to determine the favorite tall tale, fairy tale, or legendary character of each class member. Graph your results and draw conclusions.

SYNTHESIS LEVEL JOURNAL ENTRIES

a. Invent a new mythological character and create a myth about him or her.

b. Imagine you have designed a new piece of software for the English classroom. Describe it in detail.

EVALUATION LEVEL JOURNAL ENTRIES

a. Determine the most difficult topics or skills for you to learn in English. Give reasons if you can.

b. Rank the parts of speech according to complexity and importance of function.

Springboards for Student Products

1. Construct your own "Book of Lists" that contains lists of words that could help you in reading, writing, spelling, and speaking tasks. Some suggestions for word lists are:

   a. feeling words

   b. sound words

   c. transition words

   d. synonyms for overused words

   e. adventure words

   f. nature words

   g. tricky words

   h. place words

   i. suspense words

   j. favorite words

   k. science words

   l. math words

   m. social studies words

   n. descriptive words

2. Create a handbook for writers that includes pages which discuss such important learning tools and springboards as:

   a. spelling helps

   b. selected grammar terms

   c. rules for capitalization and punctuation

   d. editing skills checklist

   e. proofreaders' marks

   f. writing skills checklist

   g. book report ideas

   h. story starters

3. Prepare a language arts calendar. Write and illustrate interesting facts about popular novels, authors, poets, book characters, myths, tall tale characters, proverbs, origins of words, reference sources, fables, analogies, and poetry forms.

4. Write a series of book reviews related to a central topic such as children's picture books, joke/riddle books, puzzle books, poetry books, or art books.

5. Compose a book of letters in which you tell a story using only various types of correspondence for each page. Consider using friendly letters, thank-you notes, greeting cards, postcards, and memos as you develop your plot line.

6. Pretend the editor of a weekly newspaper has asked you to produce a Kid's Page for the first printing. Write the copy and design the format.

7. Write a CAUSE AND EFFECT booklet that answers commonly asked questions about scientific phenomena such as:

    a. What causes tornadoes?

    b. What causes air pollution?

    c. What causes erosion?

    d. What causes leaves to turn color in the fall?

    e. What causes bears to hibernate?

8. Create a travel brochure for an imaginary trip much like the Yellow Bus series of books written for young children. Consider taking a trip through an ant colony, a trip inside an active volcano, a trip to Never-Never Land, a trip through the human body, or a trip to the moon.

9. Write a short story, poem, or essay using a secret code for your alphabet.

10. Choose a popular novel and create a series of magazine advertisements using different propaganda techniques to "sell" the book to prospective readers.

11. Invent a series of "dialogues" between inanimate objects or concepts. For example, what might a pencil say to a word processor? What might a question mark say to an exclamation mark? What might a prefix say to a suffix? What might a contraction say to a conjunction?

12. Study a variety of mail-order catalogs to determine how information is organized, products are described, and wares are displayed in each. Design a unique catalog of products for a favorite fictional character. For example, what would you put in a catalog for Doctor Doolittle, for Johnny Tremain, for Amos Fortune, or for Julie of the Wolves?

13. Generate a list of 10 to 20 questions about a book of fiction that would have answers that you think everyone should know after reading a book. Test your list by trying to answer the questions about a book you have read recently.

14. Brainstorm a list of things with "holes" in them such as Swiss cheese, buttons, hula hoops, and worn-out socks. Select any five of the items from your list. Practice using personification by writing a paragraph for each item, describing "A Day in the Life of a . . . "

Springboards for Student Performances

1. Write a personal narrative describing an important incident in your life. Arrange a group of chairs in a circle and read your original narrative aloud to a group of peers. Be sure to read with expression and confidence.

2. Prepare a short skit or play based on a historical event, a scientific expedition, or a mathematical discovery. Include in your script information about the cast, signals to be used as speaking cues for the actors, and stage directions that tell the actors how to move, speak, and behave. Perform the play for a small audience and pay attention to their reactions.

3. Create a descriptive speech that uses the five senses to develop a visual image of a favorite person you know, a special place, or a possession of yours. Use a startling statement, a poignant quotation, a vivid image, an interesting anecdote, or a humorous aside to open your speech, and use something just as colorful to close it. Deliver your speech to a group of friends.

4. Collect a series of photographs or magazine illustrations on a topic of your choice and use these as a basis for composing and delivering an oral photo essay to members of your class. Be sure to arrange your illustrations or pictures in the order in which you talk about them. Be sure to give a title to your essay and captions to your visual entries.

5. Invent a tall tale character. Assume his or her identity by dressing up like the individual and giving a monologue that exaggerates everything about the character, from physical attributes and feats to adventures and accomplishments.

6. Design a puppet show storyboard that shows characters and sequential events of a plot. Remember that a storyboard does not attempt to show all of the scenes in a story, but merely serves as an outline for the major people, places, and events. Perform your puppet show so others may enjoy it.

7. Write a children's book explaining the rules of capitalization, the rules of punctuation, or the spelling of plural words. Use stick or comic strip figures in your book, and keep the explanations, examples, and exercises simple. Read the book aloud to a group of young elementary school students.

8. Design an explanatory chart to show an audience the relationships, sequences, or positions that exist within an institution, group, or collection of data. Consider any topic for this chart, from the organization of the various branches of military services, to the types of food chains in natural habitats, to the interactions of fictional characters.

9. Use one or more graphic organizers to prepare a presentation. Some graphic organizers to consider are a Concept Map, a Story Grid, a KWL (Know/Want/Learned) Chart, a Venn diagram, a Web, a Fishbone, or a Matrix. This type of presentation is designed to appeal to a person's ability to reason or to a person's ability to feel emotions. Arrange your arguments so that they: (1) ask a question and then answer it; (b) relate an anecdote, observation, or experience; and (3) state a fact or statistic.

10. Write and give a book review of a book of your choice. When preparing your review, be sure to analyze the book's setting, characterization, plot, theme, tone, point of view, and the author's style of writing. As you prepare your notes for the review, think about your reactions to the events and characters that please or bother you, your reactions to the passages that surprise or dazzle you, and the descriptions that challenge or disappoint you. Practice giving your book review in front of a mirror before giving it to an audience.

11. Do some research and prepare a mini-report on a topic you are studying in another subject area. Be sure your report contains each of the following elements:

   a. an introduction, body, and conclusion
   b. one or more direct quotations
   c. several paraphrases of important facts from a reference source
   d. summaries of important points of information

   Read your report aloud to others so that you can catch errors in grammar and punctuation before revising it.

12. Conduct an oral interview with a person of interest to you and your classmates in the school. When getting ready for your interview, prepare a "personality profile" of the individual and develop a set of potential interview questions. Write your interview results in the form of a brief news broadcast, using the "inverted pyramid" structure for this purpose. Give your broadcast over the public address system, live at a committee meeting, in person to a special interest group, or as a tape recording for the school's media center.

SAMPLE PORTFOLIO FOR
MIDDLE GRADES LANGUAGE ARTS

MY PORTFOLIO:

Interdisciplinary Unit in Language Arts

TABLE OF CONTENTS

SCIENCE ARTIFACT SELECTIONS
1. Color: My Word Association Experiment

2. Personality Similes for Science

SOCIAL STUDIES ARTIFACT SELECTION
Writing a Business Letter of Support

MATHEMATICS ARTIFACT SELECTION
A Speech to Remember

LANGUAGE ARTS ARTIFACT SELECTIONS
1. My Book of Lists

2. Using Bloom's Taxonomy to Write My Book Reports

ASSESSMENT TOOLS FOR ARTIFACTS
My Portfolio Rubric/Conference Questions

My Word Association Experiment

Color: Word Associations

PURPOSE

Every word has one or more definitions. For every word there are also "associations," or other words that the original word brings to mind. When more than one person gives a definition of a word, the definitions are often similar. But when people share their word associations, the words are often very different.

WHAT I DID

I conducted a "word association" experiment with selected members of my class. First I chose five "color words": green, red, black, white, and yellow. I wrote each word at the top of a 5" x 8" index card. I did this five times so that there were twenty-five index cards in all. I gave a set of five cards to each of five different people in my class. I instructed them to write down "all" of the words that each color word made them think of. They had just 30 seconds to write down as many words as they could for each color. I collected the cards and compared the responses. I used the results to answer the following questions:

1. How many words did each person have on his or her list?
2. Which words were on the lists of all five people?
3. Which words were on four of the five lists?
4. Which words were on three of the five lists?
5. Which words were on two of the five lists?
6. How many words were only on one person's list?
7. How many common associations were on each color word list?

My experiment results are in my portfolio file.

Reflection:

I really enjoyed doing this experiment because it was fun and interesting. I was surprised to find so many common associations for most colors, especially "green" and "white." For example, many people listed such words for "green" as grass, St. Patrick's Day, trees, beans, peas, and Green Bay Packers. One person put down the word "envy" for the idiom "green with envy." For the color "white," most people listed snow, clouds, paper, angels, sheets, and vanilla. One person put down the word "ivory" as in an elephant's tusk.

Similes

Personality Similes for Science

PURPOSE

Similes are forms of figurative language that are often found in literature, poetry, and creative writing. A simile is a comparison in which two unlike things are compared using the words **as, like,** or **than.** Similes are also found and used in other subjects, such as science. It is fun to use similes to compare people to various weather terms.

WHAT I DID

I chose seven of my friends and compared them to weather concepts that we are studying in my science class. The terms I selected were: thunder, cloud, lightning, tornado, snow, sunshine, and barometer.

JOHN IS AS LOUD AS A CLAP OF THUNDER IN A STORM.
I DON'T LIKE TO GO TO THE LIBRARY WITH HIM BECAUSE HE IS SO NOISY.

SUSAN DRIFTS THROUGH LIFE LIKE A FLOATING CLOUD. NOTHING EVER BOTHERS HER.

RAY RUNS AS QUICKLY AS A FLASH OF LIGHTNING.
HE IS SO FAST THAT HE IS THE STAR OF OUR SCHOOL'S TRACK TEAM.

TOM ACTS LIKE A TORNADO—HE IS A WHIRLWIND OF ACTIVITY FROM MORNING TO NIGHT.

JANE'S FATHER IS A DENTIST. HE MAKES HER BRUSH HER TEETH OFTEN,
EVEN AFTER EATING LUNCH AT SCHOOL. JANE'S TEETH ARE AS WHITE AS SNOW.

ANDREW IS LIKE A RAY OF SUNSHINE. HE IS FRIENDLY, UPBEAT, AND FUN TO BE AROUND.

RYAN'S MOODS GO UP AND DOWN. HE IS AS UNPREDICTABLE AS A BAROMETER.

I included my similes in my portfolio file for both science and language arts.

Reflection:

This was a neat activity and proved to me that you can practice creative writing skills in any subject, not just in English class. My friends were good sports to let me write similes about them. They agreed with what I wrote too!

Writing a
Business Letter of Support

PURPOSE

It is important to learn how to write good business letters. Knowing how to write good business letters helps students later in life when they are working in the real world. The parts of a business letter are: **Heading/return address, Date, Inside address** (name, title, organization, and address), **Salutation, Body, Closing, Signature,** and **Typed name.** One may add the word **Enclosure** if needed.

1715 Cottonwood Road
Edwards, Colorado 81632

February 8, 1995

Consumer Comment Department
P.O. Box CAMB
Battle Creek, Michigan 49016-1986

To Whom It May Concern:

I am writing to tell you how much I enjoy your breakfast cereals—especially cornflakes. I am a sixth grader at Edwards Middle School in Colorado, and I have been eating Kellogg's Cornfllakes since I was ten months old.

In my social studies class, we are studying advertising and my teacher instructed us to write a company to comment on one of their products and its packaging. I really think you do a good job in designing your cereal boxes. The things I like best about the cornflakes box are:

1. three great recipes
2. Nutrition Fact Chart
3. your invitation to submit consumer comments by calling your 800 number

Thank you for making such a nutritious and tasty cereal.

Sincerely,

Sandra Singleton

Sandra Singleton

MY BUSINESS LETTER

WHAT I DID

In social studies class we are studying the different types of propaganda used to advertise products and services. Our teacher suggested we write a business letter to the manufacturer of a product that we think is either a high-quality product or an inferior product and that uses appropriate or inappropriate ads or packaging. I chose to write to the Kellogg Corporation in Battle Creek, Michigan, because cornflakes is my favorite cereal and because I think their cereal box packaging is user-friendly. A copy of my letter is on this page. It is written in the "block" format in which every part of the letter begins at the left margin.

Reflection

I included this letter and the Kellogg Corporation's response to my letter in my portfolio file. Most of the students chose to write business letters of complaint. They wanted to tell a manufacturer everything that was wrong with a product or with an ad. I think that is a good idea, but I also think that most letters manufacturers receive are negative, and that it must be nice to get positive feedback from a customer once in a while. The sales manager of Kellogg answered my letter just one week after she received it. Business letters are easy and fun to write.

Delivering a Speech

A Speech to Remember

PURPOSE

Public speaking is a skill one can use throughout life. People often give speeches at work, though it may be as a secretary on the telephone, or as a salesperson in front of customers. There are differences between writing and speaking. In writing, good grammar and spelling are important; in speaking, tone of voice and body language are important. The way to give a good speech is to practice and prepare.

WHAT I DID

I had to give a speech in math class. I chose the topic of Problem Solving. I first developed an outline for my speech:

I. Introduction
    A. Introduce myself and state my topic.
    B. Capture my audience's attention.
       1. Ask a question.
       2. Use a prop to make a point.
       3. Tell a personal anecdote.
    C. State my beliefs or feelings about the topic.
    D. Preview the steps in problem solving.

II. Body
    A. Describe the steps in problem solving.
       1. Determine the problem.
       2. Identify relevant facts and their relationships.
       3. Specify important conditions.
       4. Choose a strategy.
       5. Solve the problem.
       6. Check the results.
    B. Discuss problem-solving strategies.
       1. Make a table or organized list.
       2. Draw a picture or use real objects.
       3. Work backwards or make it simpler.
       4. Find a pattern.
       5. Use logic by looking at cue words for addition, subtraction, multiplication, and division.

III. Conclusion
    A. Restate something important said in the introduction.
    B. Make recommendations for solving future problems.

I then used this outline to write the important points on notecards so that I had one card for each item in the outline. I used these notecards when I practiced my speech in front of a mirror and, later, in front of my mother and a group of friends. I gave my speech to the whole math class. It took approximately five minutes. I used the chalkboard as a prop for writing down key words or phrases that I wanted the people in the audience to remember.

The teacher and my peers evaluated my speech using the following criteria:

Introduction: Was it clear and interesting, and did it capture the audience's attention?

Body: Were the points and examples well-developed and were they stated in a logical order?

Conclusion: Were the ideas presented positive, thought-provoking, and helpful?

My speech is in my portfolio file. I would have gotten an "A" if I had done a better job demonstrating problem-solving strategies.

Reflection

I didn't like this assignment at all because I HATE getting up in front of a group to give a speech. I worked hours on this speech and only got a "B." It was hard to present so much information in just five minutes. I hope I don't have to give a speech again this year!

My Book of Lists

PURPOSE

Encouraging students to keep lists of everything from vocabulary words and metaphors in English to geography terms, math symbols, and mammals in other core discipline areas can be a wonderful learning tool throughout the school year. The lists can be used as resources for reference, for research, for study, for skill development in alphabetizing or classifying, and for creative expression. The lists can be written in the backs of journals, learning logs, or subject area notebooks. The lists can be carried forward from year to year with students adding to them as needed.

WHAT I DID

I purchased a special notebook in which to create a personal "Book of Lists." In this notebook I keep lists of important words, terms, concepts, ideas, and references for each of my major subject areas. My teachers gave me specific directions for developing some of the lists in my notebook, but I have included lists of my own, just for fun or for future use. Several of my friends have worked with me on my "Book of Lists" because "three or four heads" are better than one when it comes to listmaking. An outline of the lists in my notebook is on the next page. My "Book of Lists" will be part of my portfolio file.

> *Reflection*
>
> I love this project because it helps me with my classroom assignments and my homework tasks. It is almost like having a "list encyclopedia" of my own. I keep my "Book of Lists" in a three-ring binder so that I can add pages and so that I can keep my lists organized by subject area. The lists are arranged in alphabetical order within each subject area. At the bookstore I found several commercial books with lists in them and I used some of the information in my own notebook.

An Outline of Topics

My Book of Lists

These are some topics in my Book of Lists:

FINE ARTS
Artists
Composers
Famous paintings
Musical instruments
Musical symbols
Musical terms
Theater terms
Titles of favorite songs

LANGUAGE ARTS
Abbreviations
Acronyms
Analogies
Antonyms
Compound words
Grammar terms
Homonyms
Metaphors
Parts of a letter
Parts of speech words
Proofreader symbols
Puns
Rules for capitalization
Rules for forming plurals
Rules for punctuation
Similes
Slang
Suffixes
Syllables
Synonyms
Tiresome words to avoid
Tricky words to spell

SCIENCE
Animals
Birds
Chemical elements and compounds
Fishes
Flowers
Human body terms
Insects
Inventors
Minerals
Nutrition terms
Organs and systems of human body
Planets and constellations
Possible science fair projects
Solar system terms
Trees
Weather terms

MATHEMATICS
Computer terms
Famous mathematicians
Math formulas
Math shapes
Math signs and symbols
Math terms
Units of measure

MISCELLANEOUS
Study and test-taking hints
Things I don't understand
Things I want to know more about
Things I'll never forget
Things to change

LITERATURE
Authors
Book report and project ideas
Book titles
Characters in fairy tales, folktales, tall tales, legends, and myths
Fables
Famous poems
Idioms
Poets
Proverbs
Story starters

SOCIAL STUDIES
Careers
Continents of the world
Deserts of the world
Economic terms
Explorers
Famous Americans
Famous battles and wars in American history
Geography terms
Islands of the world
Languages of the world
Law terms
Longest rivers of the world
Map terms and symbols
Money of the world
Mountains of the world
Political science terms
Presidents of the United States
World leaders

Some books with lists that I recommend for other students are:

Ecology Green Pages. Nashville, TN: Incentive Publications, 1993.

Frank, Marjorie. *If You're Trying to Teach Kids How to Write . . . You've Gotta Have This Book!* Nashville, TN: Incentive Publications, 1995.

Math Yellow Pages for Students and Teachers. Nashville, TN: Incentive Publications, 1988.

Reading Yellow Pages for Students and Teachers. Nashville, TN: Incentive Publications, 1988.

Schwartz, Linda. *I Love Lists.* Santa Barbara, CA: The Learning Works, 1988.

Science Yellow Pages for Students and Teachers. Nashville, TN: Incentive Publications, 1988.

U.S. Social Studies Yellow Pages for Students and Teachers. Nashville, TN: Incentive Publications, 1993.

World Social Studies Yellow Pages for Students and Teachers. Nashville, TN: Incentive Publications, 1993.

Writing Yellow Pages for Students and Teachers. Nashville, TN: Incentive Publications, 1988.

Using Bloom's Taxonomy to Write

My Book Reports

PURPOSE

Bloom's Taxonomy is a structure for the teaching and learning of thinking skills. There are six levels in the taxonomy. They are arranged in sequence beginning with lower thinking skill levels and ending with higher thinking skill levels. These levels are, in order: Knowledge, Comprehension, Application, Analysis, Synthesis, and Evaluation. Each level is assigned a large number of verbs that can be used to write book reports.

WHAT I DID

A large chart showing Bloom's Taxonomy is posted on the bulletin board in all of our classes. I also have a mini-chart of Bloom's Taxonomy in the front of my notebook. The teacher wants us to use this chart when doing our work. This semester I had to do four book reports (one a month), and I used Bloom's taxonomy to organize my information for each report. I developed a set of Bloom tasks for each type of book report, using the chart in my notebook as a tool for selecting the best verb at each level of the taxonomy. On the next page you will see the list of things that I wrote about for each of my book reports. All four of my book reports are in my portfolio file.

Reflection

Bloom's taxonomy has been a big help as I try to organize my ideas and become a better thinker. I didn't mind writing all of these book reports because I got to decide on my own format for each report. I still find it hard to decide whether something is at the Comprehension level or the Application level, but I'm getting better at it! These are my book report outlines for this semester.

HISTORICAL FICTION BOOK REPORT

KNOWLEDGE: Identify the historical period during which this story took place.

COMPREHENSION: Describe the unique historical setting of this story.

APPLICATION: Prepare a list of events in this story that correlate with the historical events discussed in your social studies textbook.

ANALYSIS: Could the main character have really lived during this historical period? Why or why not?

SYNTHESIS: Write a dialogue between the main character and yourself. What would you both say?

EVALUATION: Decide if you would have liked to have lived during this historical period. Tell why.

BIOGRAPHY BOOK REPORT

KNOWLEDGE: Write down five facts about this person that you learned from reading the biography.

COMPREHENSION: Summarize the major events in this person's life.

APPLICATION: If you were to interview this person, what are five questions that you would want to ask him or her?

ANALYSIS: Draw conclusions. Is this person someone to be admired or not?

SYNTHESIS: Invent a nickname for this person and tell why it is a good one for him or her.

EVALUATION: Defend the biographer's choice to write about this particular individual.

NONFICTION BOOK REPORT

KNOWLEDGE: Record five pieces of information that you learned from this book.

COMPREHENSION: In your own words, define three important terms or concepts discussed in this book.

APPLICATION: Write down five questions you had about the subject of this book before reading, and discuss how these questions are answered by the author of the book.

ANALYSIS: Examine ways this book might be helpful to you and your classmates.

SYNTHESIS: Create a new title for this book.

EVALUATION: On a **1** to **5** scale, with **1** being **poor** and **5** being **excellent,** how would you rate the content and the presentation of material in this book? Be able to justify your ratings.

SCIENCE FICTION BOOK REPORT

KNOWLEDGE: Describe the major character in this book.

COMPREHENSION: List the characteristics of this book that make it a science fiction story.

APPLICATION: List in sequence five to ten major events in the story that make up the plot.

ANALYSIS: Determine which fictional parts of this story might actually become reality in the future.

SYNTHESIS: Draw a favorite scene from this book.

EVALUATION: Determine the characteristics that are common in a good science fiction book.

My Portfolio Rubric/Conference Questions

RATING SCALE

1 = I could have done better   2 = I did a good job   3 = I did a terrific job

ARTIFACTS

1. Organization and completeness of portfolio ☐ 1 ☐ 2 ☐ 3
2. Quality of artifacts selected ☐ 1 ☐ 2 ☐ 3
3. Creativity shown in work ☐ 1 ☐ 2 ☐ 3
4. Correctness of work (grammar, spelling, sentence structure, neatness, punctuation, etc.) ☐ 1 ☐ 2 ☐ 3
5. Evidence of learning concepts and/or applying skills ☐ 1 ☐ 2 ☐ 3
6. Reflection process ☐ 1 ☐ 2 ☐ 3
7. Evidence of enthusiasm and interest in assignments ☐ 1 ☐ 2 ☐ 3
8. Oral presentation of portfolio ☐ 1 ☐ 2 ☐ 3

QUESTIONS I WISH OTHERS WOULD ASK ME ABOUT MY PORTFOLIO

1. What was your favorite artifact and why?
2. What are the most interesting things you learned from your color experiment and what would you do differently next time?
3. What were the most difficult things for you to learn about grammar this year? Explain.
4. Do you think Bloom's taxonomy is one of the best learning tools for students to use? Give reasons for your answer.

GRADING SCALE
22–24 Points = A
18–21 Points = B
14–17 Points = C
10–13 Points = D
Under 10 Points = Unacceptable

My Personal Comments

I enjoyed putting together this portfolio for language arts. This is my best subject because I am strong in the Verbal/Linguistic intelligence. I liked most of our assignments this year and especially enjoyed writing My Book of Lists and writing the similes about my friends for science class. I did not enjoy giving the speech because I get nervous in front of groups even though I can write and speak well.

A Very Practical Appendix

INTERDISCIPLINARY INSTRUCTION
Planning and Carrying out a Language Arts Festival 142
Integrate Social Studies/Language Arts 144
Integrate Science/Language Arts 146
Integrate Math/Language Arts 148

PLANNING OUTLINES
Editor's Guide 150
Interdisciplinary Outline 151
Multiple Intelligences 152
Williams' Taxonomy 153
Book Report Ladder 154
Book Report Outline 155

BIBLIOGRAPHY
Annotated Bibliography 156

Integrating Instruction through Planning and Carrying out a Language Arts Festival

1. Determine the main objectives of the language arts festival, and record the objectives for use by the planners. Aside from the objectives of having fun and making people think, what will be involved in the festival? Consider activities such as writing workshops, a raffle, displays, discussion groups, possibly an appearance by a local writer or illustrator. You may wish to hold the festival in conjunction with a science and/or math fair. Include student workers in the planning of the festival.

2. Recruit volunteers (teachers and parents) who have good organizational skills and an interest in language arts to serve on the festival committee.

3. Set a time, location, and date for the festival. Determine if food or snacks will be a part of the festival.

4. Arrange for schedule, space, and school involvement with the proper administrative staff.

5. Approach a local literacy organization or the public library to see if such an organization would be willing to help sponsor the festival, if only in a small way.

6. Write guidelines for the festival. If one or more competitions will be part of the festival (i.e., a writers' contest), or if awards of any kind are to be given, include entry deadlines, categories of contests and displays, requirements for entries, judging guidelines, and award descriptions in the guidelines.

7. Draft a cover letter (to be endorsed by the principal) which introduces the festival and explains the rules.

8. Design the evaluative criteria and a corresponding evaluation form for competitions and awards.

9. Publicize the application deadline, the date of the festival, and the awards.

10. Prepare posters and bulletin board displays to be placed in the halls, the cafeteria, and in other common areas in order to generate interest throughout the school.

11. Contact and secure judges.

12. Plan the festival layout. Indoors? Outdoors? Both? Will there be concessions? Draw a floor plan for efficiency.

13. Plan, type, and reproduce the festival program.

14. Order or make certificates, ranging from entry-level certificates to prize-level certificates, all explained in the evaluative criteria.

15. Gather the necessary materials and equipment such as tables, chairs, and a portable address system.

16. Send thank-yous to parent and teacher volunteers and judges when the festival is over.

Ten High-interest Strategies/Activities to Integrate Social Studies into Language Arts

1 **Write reports or speeches and give them orally.**

Example: Prepare a short "speech to inform" that explains both the causes and results of the Spanish-American War.

2 **Express information through various forms of poetry.**

Example: Describe a geographical setting using these five poetry forms: haiku, diamante, free verse, concrete, and acrostic. Title your work "Five Ways to Look at a Landform."

3 **Use diaries or learning logs to record feelings, ideas, reflections, and observations.**

Example: After reading *The Diary of Anne Frank*, create a series of diary entries for another victim of prejudice such as a slave during Civil War times or a Vietnamese orphan during the war in Vietnam.

Example: Keep a learning log to record your feelings, reactions, and ideas about the Classic Period of Mayan History as you complete your textbook chapter and outside readings.

4 **Use children's literature and picture books.**

Example: Collect a series of picture books about people from foreign lands. Read the books and write a synopsis for each one. Determine what makes these books both appealing and informative.

5 **Read folktales, legends, myths, and tall tales.**

Example: Select a Greek or Roman mythological character to study and prepare a short picture essay that tells something about him or her.

6 **Read biographies of famous leaders, scientists, explorers, inventors, authors, artists, mathematicians, etc.**

Example: Develop an outline about the person whose biography you chose to read. Use this outline to share information about your person with members of your cooperative reading group.

7 Use the dictionary as a tool for acquiring information.

Example: Use the dictionary to define these terms related to our study of geography: island, peninsula, and isthmus.

Example: Use the dictionary to help you determine the origins of these terms associated with the computer: virus, boot up, debug, and terminal.

8 Compose original short stories.

Example: Choose one of the following topics on which to write an original story related to our study of consumer economics.

- A Bargain That Cost Me Money
- There's No Such Thing as a Free Lunch
- My Perfect Purchase
- To Buy or Not to Buy, That Is the Question!
- Buyer Beware

9 Write and send friendly or business letters.

Example: Choose one piece of correspondence from your junk mail collection, and respond to the business who sent it, expressing your thoughts and reactions to the contents of their mail.

Example: Send a friendly letter to the owner of your favorite store or retail outlet to tell him or her why you patronize the business.

10 Incorporate grammar into tasks.

Example: Browse through your textbook (or a newspaper or news magazine) and select a picture showing a current event of special interest to you. Write sentences related to the content of the picture: a declarative sentence, an interrogative sentence, an exclamatory sentence, and a sentence that gives a command.

Example: Make a list of common nouns, proper nouns, and verbs that describe or explain the Civil Rights movement.

Ten High-interest Strategies/Activities to Integrate Science into Language Arts

1 **Use the scientific method to test a hypothesis.**

Example: Create a hypothesis to find out how gender differences of students in middle grades affects their reading preferences for the different genres in literature.

2 **Identify cause and effect situations.**

Example: Develop a plan to determine how much television viewing is done daily or weekly by students in your class, and how this activity has an impact on their time and commitment to reading.

3 **Construct flow charts or diagrams to show processes for making or doing things.**

Example: Design a flow chart to show how to prepare a high-quality book report.

4 **Discover the role of science issues or topics in different reading, writing, and speaking areas of language arts.**

Example: Do some research and write a report about a major environmental topic that is a significant concern in your community.

5 **Brainstorm to generate meaningful lists of information.**

Example: Compile a glossary or list of key terms and their definitions for your study of astronomy. Use these to stage a "science spelling bee."

6 **Look for patterns and repetitive designs.**

Example: Compare number patterns in mathematics and science with rhyming patterns in various forms of poetry. How are they alike and how are they different?

7 **Use your writing skills to tell about science experiments.**

Example: Write a descriptive paragraph about a particular science experiment. Be sure your paragraph has a good topic sentence and a concluding statement.

8 **Use scientific laws or principles as the bases for biographies and reports.**

Example: Do some research and write a three-page report on photosynthesis, respiration, and transpiration as these processes relate to your study of the plant kingdom.

Example: Find out about the life of the German minerologist Friedrich Mohs, who developed the Mohs Scale for the identification of minerals by their hardness in 1822.

9 **Use concept webs or other advanced organizers to explain scientific ideas.**

Example: Complete a KWL Chart and a concept web to help you outline your speech on endangered species for language arts class.

10 **Use scientific observations to study real-world applications of language arts concepts.**

Example: View a videotape of a favorite book or movie and write a review of what you observed and felt during this visual presentation.

147

Ten High-interest Strategies/Activities to Integrate Math into Language Arts

1 **Use Venn Diagrams to compare and contrast people, places, and events.**

Example: Compare and contrast the major characters of any two novels written by Madeleine L'Engle.

2 **Construct line graphs, bar graphs, circle graphs, and pictographs.**

Example: Construct a pictograph showing the most popular genres of literature read by students in your class.

3 **Create word or story problems.**

Example: If a language arts student is expected to keep a reading log of pages read outside of class and a total of 3628 pages is recorded for the month of April, how many pages did he or she average per day?

4 **Use money and monetary systems of both the United States and other countries.**

Example: Assign a dollar value to each letter of the alphabet, with A being equal to $1.00, B equal to $2.00, C equal to $3.00, etc. Determine the dollar value of words, characters, and concepts in favorite literature or poetry passages. For example, ask students to figure out which character in the story has the most expensive name, or which metaphor in the poem has the highest value.

5 **Construct flow charts or diagrams to show processes for making or doing something.**

Example: Diagram the parts of speech in a declarative sentence or construct a flow chart to show how to classify parts of speech in a declarative sentence.

6 **Discover the role of mathematical concepts in different language arts areas.**

Example: Calculate the average number of words for each page in your short story or estimate the number of transition words that are used on each page of your short story.

7 **Conduct individual or group surveys and show results in chart form.**

Example: Survey the members of your class to determine favorite authors or favorite novels of the semester. Show your results in chart form.

8 **Use number codes to rewrite questions or answers in a reading or writing assignment.**

Example: Create and use a number code to write a series of questions and their corresponding answers concerning the chapter you have just read in your novel.

9 **Construct timelines to establish the chronology of important events.**

Example: Make a timeline to show the important sequence of events that led up to the climax of the plot in the book you are reading for this month's book-sharing session.

10 **Use topics such as measurement, shapes, probability, or symmetry to explain or demonstrate language arts terms or concepts.**

Example: Create a shape (circle, triangle, or square) poem about a language arts topic of your choice.

Example: There is a symmetry to the shapes and letters that make up some interesting vocabulary words. Identify some of these words.

Example: Explain how palindromes exhibit symmetry.

Editor's Guide

1 Have I visualized my reader? Do I understand what interests him or her?

2 Have I given careful attention to grammar, spelling, and punctuation so that my reader will experience no confusion in trying to understand my message? (Proofread your writing, and then have a person skilled in proofreading recheck for technical errors.)

3 Have I expressed my thoughts in logical, sequential order? (Number the main ideas to check this.)

4 Have I used plain, simple words in ways with which my reader will be comfortable?

5 Have I used these plain, simple words in ways that will interest my reader?

6 Have I deleted unnecessary words or phrases?

7 Have I deleted unrelated or irrelevant matter? (Underline sentences or phrases that may not relate.)

8 Have I omitted any vital or important details or information?

9 Have I avoided overworked words, phrases, and clichés?

10 Have I used the most active and "alive" words possible to express my ideas? (Look at each adjective and adverb. Ask yourself if there is a better, more interesting, more picturesque, or more precise word you might substitute.)

11 Have I used illustrations or examples to reinforce main ideas? (Make an X at places where such entries may be helpful.)

12 Have I created added interest by interspersing figures of speech, forceful repetition, or exclamations into ordinary declarative thought? (Count the number of question marks, exclamation points, quotation marks, and figures of speech you have used.)

13 Have I expressed what I honestly feel or believe, or have I been more concerned about what my teacher or my peers will think? (Use tact and sensitivity when expressing negative or unpopular feelings or ideas, but do not sacrifice clarity or effectiveness.)

14 Is my writing clear, neat, and easy to read?

15 Have I referred to the beginning in the ending and left my reader with an idea to ponder? Have I said anything to cause my reader to reconsider the subject?

From *Writing Yellow Pages for Students and Teachers,* ©1988 by Incentive Publications, Inc., Nashville, TN.
Used by permission.

Interdisciplinary Unit in Language Arts

Title: _____

Topic (or Theme): _____

Purpose

Objectives

Glossary

Introductory Activity

Activities or Projects in Related Content Areas
SOCIAL STUDIES

SCIENCE

MATH

ENRICHMENT OR EXPLORATORY

Homework or Independent Study Projects

Cooperative Learning Activity

Culminating Activity

Assessment

Integrating Language Arts to Accommodate Multiple Intelligences

Language Arts Theme: _____

	Social Studies	Science	Math
VERBAL/ LINGUISTIC			
LOGICAL/ MATHEMATICAL			
VISUAL/SPATIAL			
BODY/ KINESTHETIC			
MUSICAL/ RHYTHMICAL			
INTERPERSONAL			
INTRAPERSONAL			

NOTE: Not every square need be filled in for every topic. Just make sure there is a good content balance in each unit.

Integrating Language Arts to Accommodate Williams' Taxonomy

Language Arts Theme: _____

	Social Studies	Science	Math
FLUENCY			
FLEXIBILITY			
ORIGINALITY			
ELABORATION			
RISK TAKING			
COMPLEXITY			
CURIOSITY			
IMAGINATION			

NOTE: Not every square need be filled in for every topic. Just make sure there is a good content balance in each unit.

Book Report Ladder

Be creative when you prepare your book report—use illustrations, timelines, or whatever your imagination dictates.

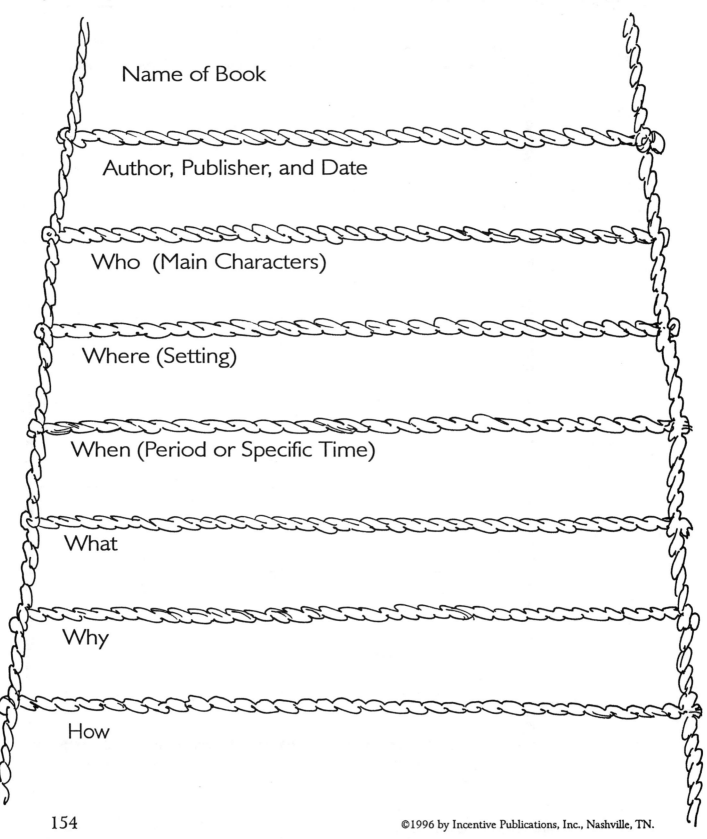

Name of Book

Author, Publisher, and Date

Who (Main Characters)

Where (Setting)

When (Period or Specific Time)

What

Why

How

Book Report Outline for Use with Any Topic

DIRECTIONS: Select a nonfiction book on the topic of your choice and use it to complete the activities below.

KNOWLEDGE
Record the answers to each of these questions:
What is the title of the book?
Who wrote the book?
When was the book published?
Where did you locate the book?

COMPREHENSION
Summarize the main ideas or facts found in the book.

APPLICATION
Select several key words or terms from the book and classify them in some way.

ANALYSIS
Compare your book with another book on the same topic. How are the books alike and how are they different?

SYNTHESIS
Suppose that you were to write a new book on this topic. Create an original book jacket for your masterpiece.

EVALUATION
Would you recommend the book to anyone else? Give three to five reasons for your answer.

Annotated Bibliography

An annotated bibliography of Incentive Publications titles selected to provide additional help for integrating instruction in language arts

Cochran, Judith. *Insights to Literature: Middle Grades.* Nashville, TN: Incentive Publications, 1990. *(Grades 6–8)*

A complete reading program designed to accompany ten widely acclaimed books.

Cook, Shirley. *Story Journal.* Nashville, TN: Incentive Publications, 1990. *(Grades 4–8)*

Seventeen wonderful books provide themes for daily journal-writing activities. Extended activities exercise creative thinking and integrate literature with the curriculum.

Crosby, Diana. *Create Your Own Class Newspaper.* Nashville, TN: Incentive Publications, 1994. *(Grades 5–8)*

A collection of reproducible activities to guide students and teachers through the process of planning, writing, and publishing a class newspaper.

Farnette, Cherrie, Imogene Forte, and Barbara Loss. *Special Kids' Stuff.* Nashville, TN: Incentive Publications, 1989. *(All grades)*

A reading and language arts supplement filled with high-interest/low vocabulary activities that help meet students' individual needs through successful learning experiences.

Forte, Imogene. *Reading Survival Skills for the Middle Grades.* Nashville, TN: Incentive Publications, 1994. *(Grades 4–7)*

Filled with exercises to improve language skills and reading proficiency, integrate reading, writing, thinking, and speaking skills, link reading to real-life experiences, and encourage efficient work habits.

Forte, Imogene and Joy MacKenzie. *Composition and Creative Writing for the Middle Grades.* Nashville, TN: Incentive Publications, 1991. *(Grades 4–7)*

This jam-packed resource will increase the fluency, flexibility, and originality in the written communication skills of your students.

—. *Writing Survival Skills for the Middle Grades.* Nashville, TN: Incentive Publications, 1991. *(Grades 4–7)*

Test-taking, résumés, business letters, and job applications are only a few of the topics covered in this essential writing skills resource.

Forte, Imogene, Marge Frank, and Joy MacKenzie. *The Kids's Stuff Book of Reading and Language Arts for the Middle Grades.* Nashville, TN: Incentive Publications, 1987. *(Grades 4–7)*

A 240-page resource loaded with creative ideas, activities, lessons, teaching strategies, and reproducibles to stimulate student interest and enhance your existing language arts program.

Forte, Imogene and Sandra Schurr. *The Definitive Middle School Guide: A Handbook for Success.* Nashville, TN: Incentive Publications, 1994. *(Grades 5–8)*

Comprehensive research-based guide provides an overview for educators, administrators, and others concerned with middle school success. Topics include interdisciplinary teaming, advisory, assessment, creative and critical thinking skills, and more.

Forte, Imogene and Sandra Schurr. *Using Favorite Picture Books to Stimulate Discussion and Encourage Critical Thinking.* Nashville, TN: Incentive Publications, 1995. *(Grades 4–8)*

This sparkling resource contains 60 thought-provoking lesson plans with accompanying activities that encourage collaboration, promote independent reading, and enhance both critical thinking and comprehension skills.

Frank, Marjorie. *Complete Writing Lessons for the Middle Grades.* Nashville, TN: Incentive Publications, 1987. *(Grades 5–8)*

An easy-to-use handbook containing an exciting assortment of teacher-directed writing lessons to encourage creativity and aid the writing process.

—. *If You're Trying to Teach Kids How to Write, You've Gotta Have This Book!* REVISED EDITION. Nashville, TN: Incentive Publications, 1995. *(All grades)*

Each bulletin board was designed to build specific math skills through suggested activities and visual stimulation. Includes clear instructions for assembly and use plus suggestions for activity extensions.

—. *Using Writing Portfolios to Enhance Instruction and Assessment.* Nashville, TN: Incentive Publications, 1994. *(All grades)*

Topics include: defining a writing portfolio, designing the portfolio, portfolio management, guidelines for evaluation, and creative portfolio activities.

Graham, Leland and Darriel Ledbetter. *How to Write a Great Research Paper.* Nashville, TN: Incentive Publications, 1995. *(Grades 6–8)*

A middle school guide written in friendly language. Includes instruction, examples, and reproducible worksheets.

Opie, Brenda and Douglas McAvinn. *Effective Language Arts Techniques for Middle Grades.* Nashville, TN: Incentive Publications, 1995. *(Grades 4–8)*

This skill-oriented resource contains both practical reproducibles and valuable activities related to book reporting, editing and proofreading, creative writing, and vocabulary enrichment.

Seguin, Marilyn. *Teaching Middle Graders to Use Process Writing Skills.* Nashville, TN: Incentive Publications, 1994. *(Grades 4–8)*

A comprehensive guide containing all the strategies, techniques, and activities needed to teach process writing skills, from pre-writing to revising.

Writing YELLOW PAGES for Students and Teachers. Nashville, TN: Incentive Publications, 1988. *(Grades 2–8)*

An amazing timesaving bank of information covering topics such as the writing process, proofreaders' marks, letter writing, and more.

Index

A

Activities
  Bloom's Taxonomy 32–41
  Calendars 69–72
  Circle of Knowledge 92–96
  Co-op Co-op 103
  Cooperative Learning 80–118
  Investigation Cards 51–66
  Jigsaw 117–118
  Multiple Intelligences 12–23
  Numbered Heads Together 105
  Round Table 107–115
  Team Learning 98–101
  Think/Pair/Share 81–85
  Three-step Interview 87–90
  Williams' Taxonomy 44–49
Annotated bibliography 156–157
Appendix 141–157
Assessment, authentic
  journal writing 122–126
  overview 120–121
  performance 120, 129–130
  portfolio 120
  product 120, 127–128
  sample portfolio 131–140

B

Be a Book Reporter 12
Bibliography 156–157
Bloom, Benjamin 30
Bloom's Taxonomy
  activities 32–41
  chart 31
  Investigation Cards 51–66
  journal writing 126
  overview 30–31
Bloom's Taxonomy of Critical
  Thought, chart 31
Book Report Ladder 154
Book reports
  Be a Book Reporter 12
  book report ladder 154
  book report outline 155

C

Calendars as an instructional tool
  calendars 69–72
  overview 67–68
Circle of Knowledge
  activities 92–96
  instructions 77
  questions/prompts 93–96
  recording sheet 92
  student directions 91

Co-op Co-op
  activities 103
  instructions 78
  recording sheet 103
  student directions 102
Cooperative learning
  activities 80–118
  overview 74–79
**Creative Writing, Thinking, and
  Speaking 22**

E

Editor's Guide 150
Editor's Guidelines 37

F

Folklore 86–90
For Fiction's Sake 41
Forming Plurals for Practice 17
Fun with Words 97–101

G

Gardner, Howard 10
Gardner's Multiple Intelligences
  activities 12–23
  overview 10–11
**Gods and Goddesses of Mount
  Olympus 102–103**
Guidelines, journal writing 122–
  123

I

Integrating instruction through
  planning and carrying out a
  language arts festival 142–
  143
Integrating language arts to
  accommodate Multiple
  Intelligences, planning
  outline 152
Integrating language arts to
  accommodate Williams'
  Taxonomy, planning outline
  153
Integrating math into language arts
  148–149
Integrating science into language
  arts 146–147
Integrating social studies into
  language arts 144–145

Interdisciplinary unit in language
  arts, planning outline 151
Interdisciplinary Unit in Language
  Arts, 131–140
**Investigate a Book of Fiction 59–
  62**
Investigate a Dictionary 63–66
Investigate the Alphabet 55–58
**Investigate the Magic of
  Language 51–54**
Investigation cards
  cards 51–66
  overview 50

J

Jigsaw
  activity 117–118
  instructions 79
  questions/prompts 117–118
  student directions 116
Join the Speaker's Bureau 16
Journal writing
  guidelines 122–123
  reflection starter statements 124
  springboards 124–126
  springboards based on Bloom's
  Taxonomy 126
  springboards for creative thinking
  125
  springboards for critical thinking
  124
Journal Writing Guidelines 122–
  123

L

Language arts festival, planning and
  carrying out 142–143
Learning Stations
  formats 25
  instructions 28
  overview 24–28
Listening In 46–47
Literary Analysis 106–115

M

Multiple Intelligences
  activities 12–23
  overview 10–11
  planning outline 152

N

News and Views 34
Numbered Heads Together
    activities 105
    instructions 78
    recording sheet 105
    student directions 104

O

Overviews
    authentic assessment 120–121
    Bloom's Taxonomy 30–31
    Cooperative Learning 74–79
    Investigation Cards 50
    Learning Stations 24–28
    Multiple Intelligences 10–11
    using calendars 67–68
    Williams' Taxonomy 42–43

P

Paragraph Power 104–105
Parts of Speech 13
Pasta Perfect 44–45
The Payoffs of Active Listening 23
Performances
    assessment 120
    springboards 129–130
Personal Publishing Project 72
Planning and carrying out a language arts festival 142–143
Planning outlines
    integrating language arts to accommodate Multiple Intelligences 152
    integrating language arts to accommodate Williams' Taxonomy 153
    interdisciplinary unit in language arts 151
Poetry 14
Poetry Pickup 33
Poetry Portraits 116–118
Portfolio
    assessment 120–121
    rubrics 121, 140
    sample 131–140
Preface 7–8
Proverbs Are Wise Sayings 21
Punctuation Rules 15

Q

Questions/prompts
    Circle of Knowledge 93–96
    Jigsaw 117–118
    Round Table 107–115
    Think/Pair/Share 81–84

R

Recording sheets
    Circle of Knowledge 92
    Co-op Co-op 103
    Jigsaw 117
    Numbered Heads Together 105
    Round Table 107–115
    Team Learning 98–101
    Think/Pair/Share 85
    Three-step Interview 88–90
Reference Referral 48–49
Round Table
    activities 107–115
    instructions 79
    student directions 106
Rubrics 121, 140

S

Sample portfolio 131–140
Speak Up 70
Springboards
    Bloom's Taxonomy 126
    creative thinking 125
    critical thinking 124
    journal writing 124–126
    student performances 129–130
    student products 127–128
    Think/Pair/Share 81–84
Springboards for Journal Writing 124–126
Storytelling 36
Strategies/activities to integrate math into language arts 148–149
Strategies/activities to integrate science into language arts 146–147
Strategies/activities to integrate social studies into language arts 144–145
Student directions
    Circle of Knowledge 91
    Co-op Co-op 102
    Jigsaw 116
    Numbered Heads Together 104
    Round Table 106
    Team Learning 97
    Think/Pair/Share 80
    Three-step Interview 86
Student performances, springboards 129–130
Student products, springboards 127–128

T

A Takeoff on Tests 35
Team Learning
    activities 98–101
    instructions 77
    student directions 97
Theory of Multiple Intelligences 10–11
Think/Pair/Share
    instructions 76
    recording sheet 85
    springboards for language arts 81–84
    student directions 80
Three-step Interview
    activities 87–90
    instructions 76
    student directions 86

U

Use Your Imagination . . . 71
Using Multiple Resources to Find Answers 18–19

V

Verb Review 32
A Very Practical Appendix 141–157
A View of You 38–40

W

Williams' Taxonomy
    activities 44–49
    overview 42–43
    planning outline 153
Williams' Taxonomy of Creative Thought, chart 43
Word Power 69
Word Processor Wisdom 20

Index entries in bold type are titles of student activities.